First published in Great Britain in 2006

First published by Ebury Press, Random House, 20 Vauxhall Bridge Road, London SW1V 2SA

Random House Australia (Pty) Limited, 20 Alfred Street, Milsons Point, Sydney, New South Wales 2061, Australia

Random House New Zealand Limited, 18 Poland Road, Glenfield, Auckland 10, New Zealand

Random House South Africa (Pty) Limited, Isle of Houghton, Corner Boundary Road & Carse O'Gowrie, Houghton, 2198, South Africa

Random House Publishers India Private Limited, 301 World Trade Tower, Hotel Intercontinental Grand Complex, Barakhamba Lane, New Delhi 110 001, India

The Random House Group Limited Reg. No. 954009
www.randomhouse.co.uk

A CIP catalogue record for this book is available from the British Library.

Art director: Vanessa-Gaye Schiff
Editor: Jane Selley
Designers: Vanessa-Gaye Schiff, Christine Wood and Two Associates

ISBN: 0 091 91073 0
ISBN-13 (from January 2007): 9780091910730

Papers used by Ebury Press are natural, recyclable products made from wood grown in sustainable forests.

Printed and bound in China by C&C Offset Printing Co. Ltd

Cathryn Thomlinson

Introduction

The story of my discovery of the remarkable world of the Faerie begins in a forest in Britain. As an architecture student, I was putting together a study of buildings from different centuries, making a comparative review of the distinctive designs. I wasn't looking forward to my first task, seventeenth-century buildings, merely because so few still exist in their original state. However, a friend told me of a broken-down cottage on her family farm that was said to date from that period, and so I gathered my camera and headed off to the countryside.

The cottage was in the depths of Winston Forest, and was inaccessible by road. Any track that had once been there was long since overgrown. The building was just visible through the festoons of ivy that now draped it, and in the overgrown garden ancient-looking plants grew wild and unkempt. Rumours that the place had once belonged to a witch, a possibility I had laughed at in the cold light of day, now seemed much more likely to be true.

Nevertheless, I had a strange feeling that my presence there was being welcomed, and I decided to explore further. The front door of the cottage had rotted away and the floorboards were rickety and mildewed, but the timeless quality of the old place, the fire-blackened grate and the dappled sunlight streaming through the window openings, captured my attention, and I photographed all I could without falling through the decayed parts of the floor.

As I knelt down to pack up my camera, I noticed an area where the floorboards had rotted away completely. In the cavity beneath was a tightly wrapped package, brown with dust and grime, and a small, elaborately carved box. I carefully pulled out the box and the bundle and, trembling with excitement, took them outside to inspect the contents.

The dark wood of the box had warped over the centuries and I couldn't open the tightly sealed lid. The bundle appeared to be some sort of manuscript, wrapped in waxed leather so brittle it crumbled when I touched it. The thick brown paper inside seemed surprisingly well preserved

in its covering of vellum. It appeared that the manuscript was written in archaic English, though I could barely decipher the cursive script. I was, however, able to make out numerous instances of the word 'Faerie'. A thrill went through me. Could this be some communication from the long-dead woman who had once inhabited this cottage?

On my return to the university, some friends in the English department looked at the document and confirmed that it was written in old English. An expert in ancient languages, Professor James Clopell, then kindly translated the manuscript into modern English for me.

Imagine my disappointment when I found that the document seemed to be nothing more than the ramblings of Good Dame Kellerman, a mad old crone obsessed with the existence of Faeries. Disappointed, I left it at the university for further study. The carved box that I had discovered was later opened up by experts in the archaeology department, and found to contain only vegetable matter (which they believed to be petals of some kind) and a portrait of a woman on a piece of parchment, sadly nearly destroyed by the passage of time.

Several years later, I was back in the area of Winston Forest. While walking through the forest I once more came to the overgrown cottage, and was again entranced by the aura of mystery that surrounded it. I took some snaps of the plants that grew both around the cottage and in the nearby wood, enchanted by the delicate flowering shrubs and trees.

I forgot about the roll of film until I was preparing to go on holiday that summer. On finding the film still in the camera, I had the pictures developed, little suspecting the surprise that lay in store for me. On one photograph of a clump of mushrooms, a human-like creature with sprouting dragonfly wings glanced mischievously up at my camera lens.

Although I was positive that I had not seen any kind of creature when I had taken the photograph, there could be no doubt that a being was present in the picture – no trick of the light could produce such an image. I cancelled my trip and headed back to the cottage, armed with several rolls of film. With the camera on a tripod, and using time-lapse photography, I captured the images you will see in this book. In observing the Faerie in their natural habitat in the garden and surrounding forest, I also proved the accuracy of every detail of the manuscript I had discovered beneath those floorboards.

While the complete document is too long to reproduce here, I have included a selection of journal entries, translated by Professor Clopell. Good Dame Kellerman's words, with their echoes of past centuries, haunt me with their truth even today.

Cathryn Thomlinson, 2006

Earthly Riches

Translator's Foreword

It is not often that I am called upon to translate a document of this nature. In general my work consists of deciphering volumes of scholarly interest only. Thus it was with some trepidation that I approached the task Cathryn Thomlinson had set me.

There can be no doubt that this manuscript is genuine. Specialized dating techniques have placed it in the mid- to late seventeenth century, and the language used by Dame Kellerman appears to be consistent with other documents of that period. Physically the manuscript is remarkably well preserved, considering the fact that it spent so many years concealed under the floorboards of a damp, ramshackle building. One can only presume that the good dame took great care in immortalizing her thoughts for future generations.

From the first word, the manuscript paints a colourful picture of the life of this woman. The fact that she wrote it at all is unusual, given the extremely low levels of literacy during the seventeenth century. Not only that, but the quality of language she uses is exceptionally advanced, indicating that she may have been born into a relatively well-to-do family, although she gives no clue as to her origins. It would appear that later in life she has fallen on hard times and is living as a pauper, with only her rich imaginings (for I find it hard to give credence to the fantastic tales she tells) for company.

I have made every effort to ensure that my translation is as meticulous as possible, and I believe that it gives an accurate insight into the life of a truly remarkable woman.

Professor James Clopell,
Professor of Ancient and Modern English,
East Bourne University

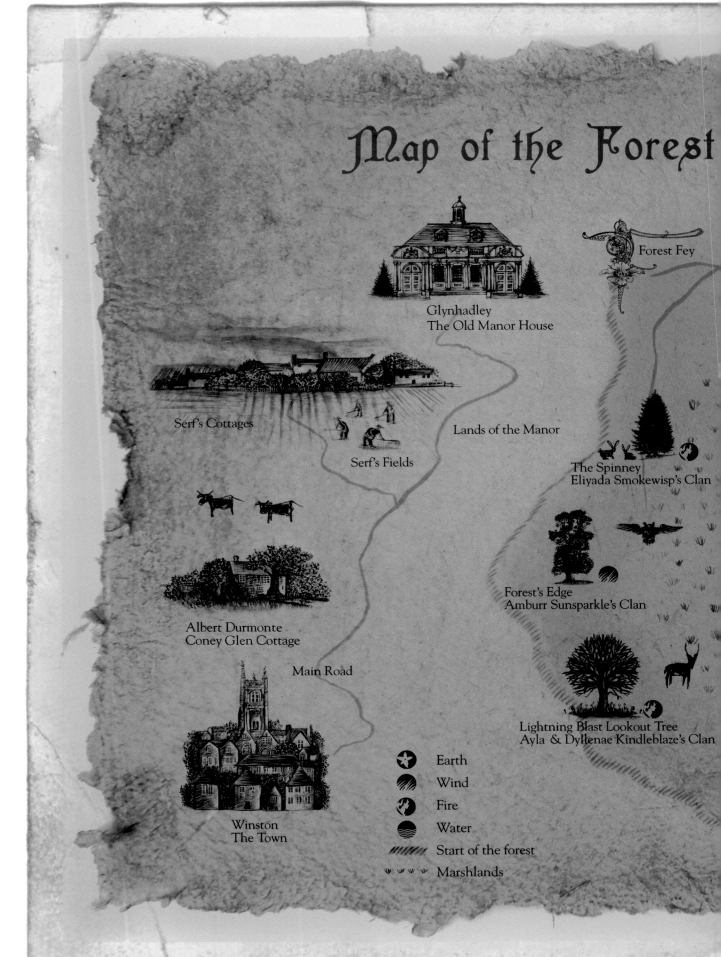

Map of the Forest

Glynhadley
The Old Manor House

Forest Fey

Serf's Cottages

Serf's Fields

Lands of the Manor

The Spinney
Eliyada Smokewisp's Clan

Forest's Edge
Amburr Sunsparkle's Clan

Albert Durmonte
Coney Glen Cottage

Main Road

Lightning Blast Lookout Tree
Ayla & Dyllenae Kindleblaze's Clan

Winston
The Town

Earth

Wind

Fire

Water

Start of the forest

Marshlands

and Faerie Clans

Haddon River

Heather Spring
Seanna Mistdance's Clan

Crystal Tears Waterfall
Ashreyel the Wise

Dragon's Breath Burn
Litanya Emberglow's Clan

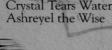
Meadowsweet Field
Jaide Leafwhirl's Clan

Pebble Pond
Dorran Spindrift's Clan

Pool of Half-Remembered Dreams
Cyanan & Alarissa Fernspray's Clan

Mossy Hollows
Brianda Dawndew's Clan

Hazel Thicket
Reyah & Bayarde Nutbrown's Clan

The Lost Loves Marshes
Karyssa & Caerlena Fenmire's Clan

Cathedral Clearing
Wisewood, The Oldest Tree
Chrystann Leafshimmer's Clan

Ivy Tendril Ridge
Baydonn Cloudweaver's Clan

Firefly Bower
Sheonnia Wildwind's Clan

Dame Kellerman's Cottage
Raelle Lavenderbalm's Clan

Memory's Wishing Well
Tirra Flamefrolic's Clan

Glossary of Main Characters

Ashreyel the Wise, the oldest of the Faerie, given power over the four elements in order to better lead the Clans

The Guardian Faeries of the Clans of Water;
Alarissa and Cyanan Fernspray, guardian of isolated pools and lakes
Brianda Dawndew, keeper of the morning dew
Seanna Mistdance, faerie of the waterfalls
Dorran Spindrift, champion of the river pools

The Guardian Faeries of the Clans of Air;
Jaide Leafwhirl, responsible for gusts of wind
Amburr Sunsparkle, cheeky faerie of the breeze
Sheonnia Wildwind, sentinel of the rough winds
Baydonn Cloudweaver, caretaker of the winds that drive the clouds

The Guardian Faeries of the Clans of Fire;
Tirra Flamefrolic, present in the first crackling flames that consume dry tinder
Eliyada Smokewisp, noble faerie of the dying fire
Dyllenae and Ayla Kindleblaze, custodians of the blazing inferno
Litanya Emberglow, fierce and warlike faerie defender of fire

The Guardian Faeries of the Clans of Earth;
Raelle Lavenderbalm, diligent in her care for herbs and garden plants
Chrystann Leafshimmer, protector of the forest
Caerlena and Karyssa Fenmire, diligent guardians of the marshes
Bayarde and Reyah Nutbrown, steadfast and dependable faeries of the thickets

The Impostor, about whose origins not much is known. He has as his mission the destruction of the Faeries, and ultimately Man

Daecien Darkmist, closest companion of Ashreyel the Wise

Saturday, 4th October 1664

I have written journals before over the years, and as I read through them now, I realize that I have had little of value to report. However, I have faithfully written down my thoughts and experiences in the hope that one day someone will find worth in the scribblings of a silly old woman.

This memoir is very different. Odd though it may be to start a journal as the year draws to a close, I feel compelled to take up my quill to pen these opening lines. Perhaps it is simply that I feel time's footsteps drawing closer. Perhaps through this chronicle I am seeking my own immortality. That is for the reader to decide, and I urge you not to judge me too harshly for seeking it, for what mortal does not?

The Lord's Day, 5th October 1664

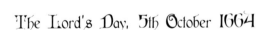

Some might frown at my setting quill to parchment on the Day of Our Lord. Yet what I have to relate will not keep for another day, and I trust that our merciful Lord will smile at an old woman's foibles. I have been considering the vanity of youth. I find it hard now to recall the time when I was a maid, but I know those years existed. I have a box of letters from my lover, scented and sprinkled with rose petals that have long since lost their colour. I have loved deeply, and known the bitterness of tragic loss.

It was this bereavement that first drew me to the forest. Its peace and loneliness suited my mood, and mirrored my feelings of tragedy and decay. Yet through the natural world and the birth of new life, I had found hope where I had thought there was none, and decided that I would never live far from a forest again. And so I settled near the small town of Winston. The bustling town itself offers little of interest to me; it is the forest that bewitches me still.

Although I have lived here for many years, and know well the rambling paths of this woodland, it seems that I never travel the same route. I wander the forest trails ceaselessly, collecting herbs or roots for my potions and simples, or merely meandering through my own world of dreams. But these journeys have also led me to a great discovery, for they have led to my crossing paths with the Faeries.

Hope of Blossoms

My first encounter with one of the fey folk, or Faeries, as they are referred to by humans, took place on a day when the rain beat down incessantly. As I made my way through the forest, I took refuge under the low-hanging branches of a tree near to a place I have always referred to as the Pool of Half-Remembered Dreams. As I sheltered there, shivering, I caught a glimpse of a face reflected in the water of the pool, a face so perfect in its aching sadness that I thought for a moment that I had lost all sense.

Not wishing to disturb the scene, yet unable to look away, I edged closer, expecting the vision to disappear with every step. Clumsily I trod on a twig, causing it to snap abruptly, and the beautiful being looked up, startled. 'Wait,' I begged, reaching out. I recognized a familiar emotion in her luminous eyes: grief. 'You are hurt, I think,' I began slowly, 'though it is not a hurt of the flesh.' I continued to move forward slowly, both hands out, approaching the being as I might a wounded animal. She stood motionless, poised as though on the brink of flight. Then, suddenly, she collapsed at the edge of the pool, overcome with heartfelt sobs.

I sat on the damp moss beside the lovely Faerie, comforting her simply with my presence. Eventually, she tentatively told me her story, and I pen it as faithfully as I can remember.

The Story of
Alarissa Fernspray

Alarissa Fernspray was her name, a Water Faerie of such beauty and grace that it could drive mortal creatures mad to look at her. Aware of this, Alarissa Fernspray had always hidden herself from human eyes, bathing in her crystal pond only when the moon was wreathed in cloud.

One day, long ago, a local nobleman, the youngest son of the famed Winston family, was thrown from his horse while hunting in the forest. He hit his head upon a rock and lay senseless for a full day, while his companions searched for him. At sundown his friends made their sorrowful way back to Glynhadley Manor, leading the young man's horse by its bridle and vowing to return the next day to continue the search.

Late that night the injured man woke and rose unsteadily to his feet. He stumbled to the pond where Alarissa Fernspray dwelled, and collapsed beside the water to drink. At that moment the clouds that covered the moon parted, and the young nobleman saw reflected in the water a creature of such beauty that he was struck dumb. Alarissa Fernspray, bathing in the clear waters of the pond, was no less surprised, but the man was strong and noble to behold. Love for the mortal leapt into her spirit, and although she hid herself in the thickets of the forest and refused to speak to him, despite his pleas – for such a love was forbidden her – her Faerie heart ached for him.

The next day, while his friends searched the forest, the young man lay unmoving by the pool, thinking only of what he had glimpsed and then lost. For days, the youth did not rouse himself to eat, merely sipping water from the pool, until he became a mere shadow of the strong man he had once been. Alarissa Fernspray was torn between wanting to reach for him and obeying the laws that forbade love between two such disparate creatures as themselves.

Eventually it seemed that the young man was near death. His cheeks were hollow, his eyes dull and indifferent. What harm could it do, reasoned Alarissa Fernspray as she tiptoed closer to the dying man, to hold his head in her lap and soothe his passing into the next world? She sat down beside him, tenderly supporting his head, and looked deep into his failing eyes. At that moment, a small spark was kindled in the young nobleman: the will to live. With a mixture of despair and a certain fierce joy, Alarissa saw it and knew she could not turn from the path she had taken. As time passed, she fed him berries and bathed his fevered brow with water until he was vigorous and healthy once more.

overleaf: Silver Shadows in the Thicket

The young man never returned to the world of mortals. His friends had long since stopped searching, presuming him dead, and perhaps it was better for them to believe so. Alarissa Fernspray spent the years of his mortal life with him, a joyous time, but one that passed all too swiftly. All humans are appointed a time to die, and the Faerie possess no magical potion for the prolonging of years. Alarissa's punishment was to see her beloved slipping away from her, first into the aches and pains of old age, and finally into death, where immortals cannot follow.

When he laid down his head for the last time on the mossy bank of the pool where they had been lovers, Alarissa's grief was terrible to behold. The cries of Alarissa Fernspray rang through the forest, breaking the hearts of all who heard them.

The Lord's Day, 12th October 1664

My duties in the village have kept me from the forest paths these past days, and my frustrated mind has been preoccupied with the Faerie. She haunts my dreams and waking moments alike, for I am fascinated by her beauty, and overcome with sorrow for her loss. But today I journeyed to the pond where I first met Alarissa Fernspray. The air around me was redolent with the aroma of flowers, soft with the droning of bees, and I knew she was there, watching me from her perch among the forest ferns.

'Alarissa!' I called, half expecting our previous meeting to have been merely a fantastic dream. Yet she came to my bidding, for now that she had told me her true name, we were inextricably bound together. She approached, graceful as a reed blowing in a gentle wind, her feet skimming the surface of the clear pond. I noted with concern that her previously vibrant face was now wan and colourless. I exclaimed at the change in her appearance, and she explained, in her melodious voice, 'It has been said that Faeries are immortal, and this is partly true. But if a Faerie chooses to merge her existence with that of a mortal being, whether plant or animal, her life will come to an end with the passing of that organism. Thus, a Faerie who has lived for years within the branches of a mighty oak will pine and die within a few days of her plant being cut down.'

'Do not follow him into dust,' I begged. Her eyes filled with crystal tears that spilled over to

Twilight Echoes

run down her smooth cheeks. I did not know what to say, but then the spark of an idea suddenly came to me.

'Mortal man, always suspicious, believes such falsehoods about the Faerie,' I began. 'Who else, he reasons, could be responsible for a barn set alight, a hole in a good rug in front of a glowing fire, or milk turned inexplicably sour overnight? But mortal man knows nothing of the true nature of the fair folk,' I continued. 'If you taught me the truth, I would make it my duty to enlighten those with whom I come into contact.'

I felt that, in saving this glorious creature from the void even for a few days, my life would acquire some meaning. She shrugged her shoulders in a gesture of hopelessness, yet I could see that the idea had taken root. I knew it would take time to convince her though, and so I took my leave and returned to my cottage, wondering whether it would be the last time I saw the Faerie. Even now, at home, my mind is filled with anguish, and I fear that sleep will not come soon this night.

Monday, 13th October 1664

After a few dream-tossed hours, I rose and in the still, cold light of dawn made my way to the Pool of Half-Remembered Dreams. The world was hushed, with even the birds' songs sounding muted, and the grasses that slapped my skirts seemed wet with tears.

As I approached the pool, once alive with magic, the place now appeared desolate and deserted. My heart was in my throat as I gathered courage to speak. 'Alarissa!' I called, though I expected no answer. For an interminable moment all was still. A frog dived from a lilypad with a splash that made me start. Then I heard her voice, soft and tired and filled with pain.

'Why do you seek me, mortal woman? Leave me to fade in peace, my spirit to merge with that of the world.'

My fear of losing her made me bold. 'I have much to learn, Alarissa Fernspray. I would have you teach me.'

Suddenly she stood before me, her fathomless eyes gazing deeply into my aged ones.

'It will cost you everything,' she said, her tone intense. 'Your own folk will not believe you, and will call you mad. Your grasp on the world in which you live will weaken; the Faerie life will become your reality. Your realm is not ready to understand ours, and its hostility will alter your perception of it, turning beauty into ashes, loveliness into dust. Are you prepared?'

I thought for a while. 'Alarissa,' I replied. 'I know your fear is for me, and for what my life may become when its boundaries merge with those of your world. Yet in all my years on this earth, I have never felt more alive than I do at this moment. I know, as surely as I have known anything in my life, that this is what I want.'

Her luminous eyes searched mine intently. 'So be it,' she whispered, but her face was sad. 'Meet with me at sunrise tomorrow and we shall begin.'

In a cloud of golden sparkles she disappeared from sight, leaving me open-mouthed in wonder, and with a huge sense of relief in my breast.

Tuesday, 14th October 1664

'A swirl of golden dust motes, disappearing too swiftly for the eye to comprehend, may signify the birth of a new Faerie. For although Faeries are immortal, new Faeries are created from the essence of light interacting with the magic of the earth. Mortal life forms consist of spirit clothed in flesh. A Faerie, however, consists solely of spirit, the purest essence of the life force that was breathed into creation at the beginning of time.'

Thus began my lessons of the fair folk. Alarissa was an excellent teacher and in her melodious voice she gently laid to rest the myths of the Faerie to which we mortals have clung for so long. From the birth of time there have existed beings on this earth of which we are not aware. Many things we do not understand are simply hidden from our comprehension.

And seated comfortably on the moss near the Pool of Half-Remembered Dreams, Alarissa described to me the birth of the first Faerie.

23

Karyssa Fenmire

The Birth of the Faerie

At the beginning of time, the Supreme Source and Maker of All Life separated the light from the darkness, moulded the earth and divided the sea from the land. He fashioned every plant and living creature. Then, to crown his creation, from the dust of the earth he fashioned a being like him in spirit to look after his world, a creature that would understand and even love him. With tenderness he gathered this limp being into his arms and breathed life into its nostrils.

This being was Man and, far from loving the creator of all these earthly wonders, Man turned his back on the one who had made him.

And so the Supreme Source and Maker of All Life said, 'I have made Man, and in his pride he has turned away from me. Who will guard the animals I have created? Who will cultivate the plants and encourage the living things to grow? Who will guide Man back to me, before he dies and is lost in the blackness of his ignorance for ever?'

The angels who surrounded him mourned, and the sun set on Man as he wandered the earth. Then the Supreme Source stretched out his hand. From the fire of the sunset, from the crystal waters that flowed in the mountains and the crash of the sea, from the scent of the evening flowers and the rich loam of the earth, from the sweet breath of the wind and the gossamer wisps of the clouds, he created a being, beautiful, strong and courageous. A Faerie.

He told this first Faerie: 'Man has dominion over the earth, and all thereon, but the earth has need of guardians to protect her from him. I fear that where Man was created to revere and protect, he will destroy. Where he was created to invent and love, he will crush and kill. Guard my realm and teach Man to cherish, sustain and nurture through your example. Show him the beauty of nature so that he will return to the Supreme Source who conceived it.'

Then he placed the spark of life within the Faerie, a spark that would never fade. 'This spark makes you different from Man,' he declared. 'With it, you will live a day while a man lives his life. The cycles of Man's history will pass you many times, so that you might learn the patterns of his future, and show him how to fulfil his potential. Do not fail me.'

With these words he put the Faerie, a being composed of the four elements, on the earth.

Alarissa's voice had painted a picture of such magnificence that I found it difficult to return to the damp moss beside the forest pool. I shook myself and headed home as the sun was setting. As I walked, I thought about the Faerie's words, and I grieved for Man.

Baydonn Cloudweaver

Wednesday, 15th October 1664

'I have explained that the Faerie were created from the four elements that make up this world,' continued Alarissa Fernspray the following morning. She was sitting on a mat of lush grass at the side of the Pool of Half-Remembered Dreams. 'My telling of the story challenged me to remember my purpose on this earth, the reason for which I was created,' she added softly. I could see from her glowing eyes that she had more to say, and I leaned forward and listened eagerly as she folded her hands in her lap and continued with her lesson for the day.

The Formation of the Faerie Clans

When the Faerie first appeared on the earth, the Four Elemental Clans were not yet formed. Perhaps you did not know of the clan system amongst the Faerie? I will tell more of this later. Suffice it to say that individual Faeries did what little they could to protect the earth and her animals and plants, and they performed these duties largely alone. Meanwhile, Man grew numerous, ever stronger and more destructive, plundering the forests for wood for his fire and land for his crops, polluting the clear-flowing streams with his wastes.

As time passed, the Faerie grew weary with nurturing the elements, and it was then that the first Great Council of Faeries was summoned. Faeries from all over the earth assembled to discuss what should be done to curb Man's destruction of the realm that gave him life. They met under a sacred tree named Wisewood, one of the first trees to grow on the face of the earth. Its gnarled bark formed a fitting background to the solemnity of the occasion. However, unknown to the Faeries, an intruder, a dark deceiver, took his place in their midst, one who opposed the Supreme

Raelle Lavenderbalm

Source and Maker of All Life and wished to see the desecration of all his handiwork. This Impostor had cloaked himself in beauty, and his presence was such that even the oldest Faerie could not help but be intrigued by him.

As the Faeries debated their problem, the intruder sat silent, listening to all that was said. Eventually all discussion was ended but no satisfactory conclusion had been reached. It was then that the Impostor rose dramatically to his feet. With his cloak of poison ivy swirling majestically around his ankles, the mere force of his presence quietened the gathered Faeries. His face had such a dark and brooding beauty that all looked upon him with awe, and fell reverently silent.

In a voice that evoked the power of summer thunder over a desert, the Impostor began to speak.

'Since the creation of this wondrous planet, nothing has marred its perfection. The majestic sun rises and falls, all seasons are regulated, each tide is preordained, each phase of the moon held in a delicate balance. The forests and meadows bring forth all that is wholesome and the sea provides limitless bounty.'

The Faeries were overwhelmed and gave the Impostor their rapt attention as he continued smoothly.

'Yet on the face of this great world there is one blight. One affliction so dire that in time it will seek to destroy the very world from which it draws sustenance. I refer, of course, to Man. He who is called Crown of Creation, but who is little more than a worm in the dust before our power and might.'

At this there was a great outcry from the assembled Faeries, for they knew that their mission on this earth was not to supplant Man, but to lead him back to a love of the Supreme Source. The Impostor held up his hand for silence.

'It is my suggestion that if Man were removed from the face of the earth, it would be free to prosper, and the true beauty of creation would be thus revealed.'

At this many of the Faeries looked uncertain, for the Impostor's words held glimmers of truth. He pressed his advantage.

'Was it not the intention of the Supreme Source and Maker of All Life to better his creation of Man by his creation of the Faerie? Did he not wish that the Faerie should supersede Man, bringing the world to fertility and richness once more?'

Such was his persuasiveness that many of the Faeries leapt to their feet in agreement, and in their weariness at protecting the earth from the depredations of Man, they took his words to heart, calling for swift means to end Man's domination of the earth.

In all the tumultuous excitement only two figures remained still. The first was the Impostor, who stared maliciously at the havoc that he had brought about. The second was Ashreyel, the oldest of the Faeries, into whom the Supreme Source and Maker of All Life had placed the first spark of life. His heart deeply troubled, he faced the Impostor in silence, holding up his hands for quiet. Gradually the Faeries hushed.

'Your words are true, stranger,' Ashreyel began. 'None here can deny that Man destroys and spoils for his own greed. He pollutes the rivers and seas, he cuts down the sacred trees and burns them in his fires, he murders the animals in order to adorn himself with their skins.'

At this, many of the Faerie nodded and muttered in agreement. Again Ashreyel held up his hands before continuing.

'But that is only part of the truth. In my many years as witness to Man's existence on the earth, I have also observed acts of great beauty and boundless love. I have seen women defy mounted armies or ravenous beasts for the sake of their children. I have seen rich men offer food to beggars. I have seen starving men release injured animals from traps when their hunger would have been satisfied by the animal's flesh. I have seen Man strive against nature in the fields he has sown, and I have seen him reap his reward with the sweat of his brow. I have seen Man love and rejoice. I have seen him dance and I have seen him mourn the passing of life. I have even seen Man come to know God.'

The face of the Impostor turned deathly pale at these words. Ashreyel continued without pause.

'Thus it is that I speak the truth, stranger, when I say that Man has a chance of redemption. The Faerie through their guardianship must inspire him to create, to nurture and to love. This is our appointed task. We must try to accomplish it, and thereby delight the Supreme Source and Maker of All Life who fashioned us for this purpose.'

At this, the Impostor rose into the air with a shriek. His poison-green cloak fluttered away to reveal dark, scaly wings, tipped with claws red as blood. His handsome face fixed itself in a terrible snarl of fury.

'Fools!' he shrieked. 'I offer you the world as your dominion, to rule it as you see fit. I ask only

that you bow to my will. I will yet see your words of redemption fall to dust.'

With a mighty noise of crashing thunder he swirled from the gathering, trailing in his wake a number of the Faerie who had been pierced by his words. When the last of them had taken their leave, Ashreyel looked about him in sorrow at those that remained.

'There are few of us left here to accomplish the tasks that have been set before us,' he admitted sadly. 'Thus I propose the following solution. Let us establish clans that will oversee the functioning of the four elements of fire, earth, air and water. Each clan shall be guardian to its own element. And I will petition the Supreme Source and Maker of All Life to create more Faeries, that we might accomplish his desires for the world.'

The Faeries dispersed from their gathering with heavy hearts, leaving Ashreyel, the oldest Faerie, alone.

When Alarissa Fernspray had ended her tale, questions were whirling through my mind, but she dismissed my queries with a wry smile.

'If I reveal all now, what then will be left for the morrow?' she asked with a laugh, and it gladdened my heart to hear it, even though I could barely contain my impatience. In an amused voice she continued, 'I will add a small crumb to your feast. Each Faerie is assigned responsibility for, though not dominion over, a specific element of the firmament, whether air, water, earth or fire. We care for and shelter from harm all who dwell within our chosen realm, although we are not as powerful against damage and destruction as some would believe. One ruthless human action can leave us mourning a cherished animal friend, laying it to rest with tenderness and tears.'

Once again I walked home, taking in the evening air, and pondering her story. I recalled a time when fire swept through the village and Good Dame Small organised the women to provide for the families left bereft, while the men banded together and built anew. It struck me that the flames of tribulation burn away the dross, and leave only the burnished gold.

Monday, 20th October 1664

The weather has turned colder, and I can feel the bite of winter in every gust of wind that whistles under the door of my cottage. The weather confines me here with nothing but my journals and the concoction of potions to keep me occupied. And Mog of course – how could I forget my poor darling cat winding his way between my ankles as I sit to write?

I worry for Alarissa. Not for her survival of the winter to come, for I know that she has endured for many hundreds of seasons beside the Pool of Half-Remembered Dreams. But in linking her life to mine, I feel I have given her purpose again, and I do not want her to think that I have abandoned her.

But for now, time drags. From my hidey-hole beneath the floorboards, I withdraw a wooden box. I feel a pang of nostalgia as I open it and the smell of long-dried rose petals rises. It is the scent of my lost youth, of the girl I once was. Beneath the faded, rustling petals, my hand alights on a scrap of parchment tied with a piece of ribbon that I once wore in my hair. Carefully I untie the knots, smoothing the yellowing piece of leather.

It is a sketch, in charcoal, of a young girl. I can scarce believe that she and I are one and the same. The painter who captured the smoky passion in my eyes was a young man named Jonathan Shawe. Our love burned bright and hot: relishing our stolen kisses and secret meetings, we made plans to marry and spend the rest of our lives together.

I vividly remember the day he gave me the portrait. He had worked on it for many nights, painstakingly drawing my likeness by the light of a single candle. The small roll of vellum was bound with the ribbon he had teasingly stolen from my hair. 'I have to go away for a short while,' he told me as he pressed it into my hand, and a strange premonition flooded me. He planned to travel to London and make his fortune as an artist, so that we had the means to live in comfort for the rest of our days. As he turned to leave, I wanted to run after him and beg him to stay, but my pride would not let me and I sent him on his way with a smile.

Less than six months later he returned, but the handsome youth of my remembrance had vanished. He was gaunt and thin, a sheen of sweat covering the unhealthy pallor of his skin. The villagers feared he was carrying the plague, and closed their doors to him. Against the orders of my master, I hid my love in the sweet hay of the cattle byre, and there I laboured, with all the knowledge of herbs and simples at my command, to save him. For a while it seemed as though he would rally:

his fever broke and he looked on me with lucid eyes, motioning me to his knapsack on the floor. In it I found a scrap of parchment addressed to me, but I cast it aside impatiently, stroking his brow and assuring him that I loved him. It was then that I saw the small blister on his brow. It was the pox.

Within a day, he was riddled with the disgusting disease, and there was nothing I could do to ease the spasms of pain that racked him. Oblivious to my own health, I stayed by his side as he slipped gradually away. In its final repose, his face regained the contours with which I was so familiar. It eased my heart a little, knowing that he no longer suffered.

I buried him myself, for I knew that no one else would come near his body for fear of the terrible contagion. I dug a shallow grave in the meadow where we used to meet, and the grass still springs up there to remind me of his irrepressible spirit. I longed to follow him into death, but God ignored my pleas.

It was many days before I could bring myself to read his final note to me. As I sit at my table now, I take it from the box. It is my greatest treasure, a poem of love lost, of regret, and of resignation, and as I read it once more, I know, as I knew then, that he understood that he would die. He knew, and he came back to show me he had not deserted me.

After he died I knew there could never be anyone else for me. Others have tried, the most recent of these being dear old Albert Durmonte, who has called on me once a week for the past fifteen years, always bearing a gift. We have an easy friendship now, and I have the impression that he is as content with the situation as I am. I hear his footsteps on the garden path now, and so I must hurry to put away my precious treasures. There are some things in life that are not meant to be shared.

A cold wind blustered as I made my way to the Pool of Half-Remembered Dreams in the pale light of morning, but I was so curious to hear more of Alarissa's tales that I paid little heed to the inclement weather – time is short, and there is still too much to learn, too much to write.

I greeted Alarissa courteously, then launched into the questions that had been troubling me since the weather forced me indoors. She laughed her tinkling laugh.

'Hush, and I will tell you all you desire to know!' she retorted, and without further ado, settled herself to continue her story.

Alarissa Fernspray

The Tale of Ashreyel and the Supreme Source

After the desertion of many of the Faeries, Ashreyel left the sacred tree with a heavy heart, determined to make his way to the Maker of All Life. As the oldest and wisest of the Faeries, he felt responsible for the defection to the side of evil, and it was with terrible dread that he began his journey across hills, forests and deserts to the home of the Supreme Source: the Mountain of Sanctity.

As a Faerie, Ashreyel could have made the journey in the blink of an eye, for Faeries are composed of spirit and are not bound by the physical laws that govern the world of men. However, he chose a long and difficult path, hoping that in the trials of his journey he would find absolution and a measure of peace. The sun burned him by day and cold winds froze him by night, and he longed to give up his quest. But the dawn of each day gave him renewed hope and vigour, and he pressed on.

After countless arduous days he arrived at the Mountain of Sanctity. It stood like a lone sentinel against the sky, its brooding presence dominating the landscape. Gathering more courage than he had thought he possessed, Ashreyel climbed the mountain, feeling with each step as though he were weighted down with lead. Trembling, he entered the place of the Supreme Source's authority and majesty on earth, and prostrated himself before him.

'Ashreyel!' The Supreme Source called his name softly and raised him up gently to face him. 'Why is it that you mourn? Is the world I have created not beautiful in all ways? Do the flowering

bushes not fragrance the air with their perfume? Do the animals not delight your spirit with their frolics? What is amiss?'

Ashreyel turned and gazed out at the plains spreading before him like an elaborate carpet of jewels. The sun climbed high in a sky of azure blue and birds danced across the heavens.

'Truly, Great One, there is nothing in all your creation that is defective. It is perfect in every way. Yet on your earth there is one who seeks to destroy, who seeks to taint your magnificent creation. And he has persuaded some of the Faeries to turn to his ways of evil, as he once persuaded Man. I have failed you.' Ashreyel's voice was desolate.

The Supreme Source and Maker of All Life smiled sadly. 'You know, Ashreyel, that I see all things,' he replied. 'I know that the Impostor dwells amongst men, and that he seeks to pervert my design with his lies. Yet at his creation I offered Man the freedom to choose, and with that freedom goes responsibility for those choices. So too with the Faerie.' He held out one closed fist. 'Choose,' he said.

Ashreyel was confused. 'I cannot choose,' he said slowly, 'because there is only one option.'

'Precisely. So what kind of a choice would that be?' Both were silent for some time. 'And as such,' continued the Supreme Source, 'how can you be responsible for the choices made by others? That thought is unworthy of you, Ashreyel.'

Ashreyel was chastened. After a while he said, 'The Faerie are too few now to do the work you have set us. I have come to beg for your assistance.'

'Tell me, Ashreyel,' asked the Supreme Source, 'why did you journey so far to meet with me? You know that I am there beside you for all time, yet still you chose to travel across hills and mountains, forests and deserts, to my Mountain of Sanctity.'

Ashreyel thought for some time. 'In enduring the journey I found peace. In the hardships I encountered I found steadfastness. With each step I acquired the resolve and courage to face you with my failure. I was able to observe the things you have created and take joy in them. But why do you ask?'

'I have chosen to grant your request, Ashreyel,' said the Great One, holding up a hand to stay Ashreyel's declarations of gratitude. 'However, the Faeries added to your number must be hardened by the resolve that held you to your journey. They must be tempered with the fires of disappointment and trial, until their courage shines bright and true. Only then will they be able to withstand the onslaught of the Impostor which, be assured, will come.'

Ashreyel considered these words fearfully. 'How is this to be achieved then, Great One?'

'Your fate is to be forever bound to that of Man, as it was in the beginning,' the Supreme Source declared. 'As you are responsible for leading Man back to me, so he will be responsible for the initiation of new Faeries to guide him, in a never-ending cycle.' On the ground in front of him he spread out the elements from which the Faerie were fashioned: a limpid pool of water, a glowing fire, a wispy feather and a heap of loamy soil. 'Behold, the creation of a new Faerie,' intoned the Supreme Source.

Ashreyel watched the components with interest. Eventually, after what seemed like an eternity, he raised his eyes in puzzlement. 'I don't understand,' he admitted. 'Where is the Faerie?'

'Patience, Ashreyel,' cautioned the Great One.

Suddenly Ashreyel perceived a small movement. Fragments of each element rose slowly and coalesced, whirling around in a golden shower of sparks until at last, perfectly formed, a Faerie lay unmoving before the feet of the Supreme Source and Maker of All Life.

'Why did it take such a long time?' asked Ashreyel.

'For each virtuous deed of Man, one element is added to the blend that will finally make up the Faerie. Man's destiny will forever be tied to that of the Faerie, his choices will determine your prosperity, and in turn, your abundance on the earth will determine Man's fate. In this way, the Faerie will never be tempted to assume that Man is less than they, simply because of the finite nature of his life. He is the Crown of my Creation and will ever remain so.'

Ashreyel glanced at the Faerie lying motionless on the ground. He gestured towards her with his staff. 'What will rouse her to life?' he asked.

'The power over life and death is mine alone,' said the Great One. 'It is I who place the first spark of life in a being, and it is I who call that spirit home.' With these words, he bent and placed an iridescent spark of life within the Faerie's breast. At once she burst joyously into life. 'Go,' he told her, 'and make the earth your home and your responsibility, never forgetting that your duty is to Man and to leading him back to me through the glory of creation.'

As the Faerie sped off, Ashreyel marvelled at what had happened. 'Truly your wisdom is without bounds,' he said, 'and your mercy without measure.'

The Supreme Source and Maker of All Life looked sad. 'Man lives his short life tempestuously, and then dies regretting the things he failed to achieve. This is the greatest

40

River of Daydreams

deception of the Impostor: that there is all the time in the world, and yet far too little time to make a difference.'

They were silent for a while. Then the Great One placed his mighty hand on Ashreyel's brow. 'Each Faerie has power over his or her particular element, but in you I place greater power. You will call on all elements, and they will be yours to command. Are you ready for this task?'

'Lord, I am not!' protested Ashreyel. 'I have failed you before. I beg you to give this duty to another.'

The Supreme Source and Maker of All Life smiled, and it was a smile filled with the glory of a blazing summer's day and the freshness of a thunderstorm in the mountains.

'If you had felt worthy to accept this task, Ashreyel, I would have known you were not. Go now, beloved, and do as I have commanded you.'

Bemused, Ashreyel made his way down the slopes of the Mountain of Sanctity and began the long journey back towards the sacred tree where the Faeries anxiously awaited him.

Thursday, 23rd October 1664

Alarissa's tale of Ashreyel and the Supreme Source had left both her and me overcome with emotion. I marvelled at the tightness of the bond between Faerie and Man, and at the same time wondered at Man's lack of regard for his end of the bargain. This morning, despite the bitter cold, I felt compelled to return to the pool and hear more, determined to note it all down before my life draws to a close.

'There is much I have not told you of the Guardians of the clans,' Alarissa said as we sat in the weak sunlight. I was shivering so hard that my teeth were chattering, but lately I have been feeling an urgency to learn as much as I can, and despite the weather I continue to come and sit beside her pool. It seems as though my life is rushing towards its end, and the responsibility to note down all I can before it comes to its final conclusion weighs heavily on my heart.

'I am curious to know of the Guardians, for you have told me of the seventeen that remained after the Great Falling Away of the Faerie. But of who they are, and what they do, you have told me nothing,' I replied.

'Let us set to rights that oversight. I will tell you of the Faeries of the element of Water,' and Alarissa Fernspray continued with her tale.

The Water Faeries

All Faeries are attracted by clear, pure-flowing water. As tears, water enhances emotion; as rain it imparts life to arid places, giving lushness and freshness; as the ocean it embodies strength

Seanna Mistdance

and changeability. Water has the same effects on the Faerie spirit, and it serves as a cleansing essence, washing away impurities.

Water Faeries take special responsibility for their chosen element. Our preferred habitats are burbling brooks and mirrored lakes. Our task is to guard the waterways of the world, for, in its never-ending cycle of renewal, water represents life and hope for mankind.

Four Guardians have been appointed for each element, and each has a different commission. Among the Water Faeries are Brianda Dawndew and her clan, who take responsibility for the morning dew that falls to the earth. Theirs is the clan of mists and early mornings, of the smells of loamy earth and bedewed grass. They haunt the humble hills and lofty mountain crags, where the rising sun illuminates the mist-shrouded valleys and the copper and purple heather glistens with pearls of dew. They take delight in the drops that are suspended in spiders' webs, making each fine thread sparkle like a necklace of diamonds. In nature, the Dawndews are soft and gentle, like the dew falling on summer grass, effervescent like the first rays of sun netted in the frost that rimes a fallen leaf.

Seanna Mistdance's clan makes its home in the shimmering droplets that spray from waterfalls as they tumble over mossy boulders. It is a cool, green world of caves behind cascading curtains of water, of dripping verdant ferns, swift currents and rapid-tossed sprays. Light as the froth and foam on the burbling water, the Mistdances are caught up on the wind, and at night they dance on mossy emerald banks and whirl to the music of the cataracts. They are exuberant and fluid, quick-witted and fond of adventure.

Cyanan Fernspray

The clan of Dorran Spindrift has its abode in the deep, still pools between the swiftly flowing sections of the river; where tree branches meet across glassy water; and where roots drink deep of the river's bounty, of herbs and minerals from the earth, of water heady as wine. The rich smells of wet banks and earthy loam, of willow leaves drooping into clear water and dank cold places that seldom see the sun are this clan's delight. Here fish lay their myriad jewel-like eggs in the stillness of the shallows; wading birds build their haphazard nests and raise their chicks on the moss-grown banks. The Spindrifts are powerful swimmers, freeing small fish from hooks and guarding the nests of water birds from the feet of unheeding fishermen.

My own clan, that of the Fernsprays, is the clan of the small isolated pools and lakes that provide the forest animals with water. With my bond-sister Cyanan, I rule a clan of flowering trees and shrubs close to mirrored ponds and lakes, a clan of scattered petals on watery reflections, where frogs splash and leap and dragonflies dart and lay their precious eggs. Ferns drink in their own reflections as they bow low over the pools; small birds chirp and flutter in the shallows, scattering iridescent beads of water until their plumage is glossy. The scent of blooming trees and grass heavy with seed meanders across the glassy waters. In winter, it is a world festooned with icicles, delicate traceries like spun sugar banding the branches and sending tendrils of ice across the surface of the ponds. Frogs and fish dive deep into the mud, there to sleep away the months until spring returns.

So each clan of Water fulfils its duties and protects the nature under its care.

Monday, 27th October 1664

When I next saw her, Alarissa Fernspray was sitting by the side of her pool, gazing at her image in the still water. Quietly I approached until my own reflection appeared in the water next to hers. She did not move, and for a while I thought that she had not noticed me. Then she spoke, and her tone was so harsh a flock of starlings in a nearby tree started chirping raucously.

'I have aged,' she said bitterly.

'Faeries do not age,' I countered, 'and you are as beautiful as the day I first saw you.'

'I fear that my time of mourning has altered me irreparably,' she whispered, 'and I no longer yearn for the oblivion of death as I once did. You have changed that,' she said, her luminous eyes gazing at me almost accusingly.

'Beauty is just a cloak,' she went on. 'It is not of our making, but something merely wrapped around us at our creation. Man or Faerie, what right do we have to be proud of that which we ourselves have not created? To despise those who are seen as ugly, since it is not their choice, but their burden?'

I could see that Alarissa was preparing to tell a story, and I sank to the moss beside her.

The Tale of Dyllenae Kindleblaze

Ashreyel the Wise was passing through Winston Forest one day on his travels. Since that first council at the Wisewood Tree he visited all of the Faeries often, to pass on news of their kin in distant lands. As he passed the Lightning Blast Lookout Tree, he caught a glimpse of Dyllenae Kindleblaze, the guardian of one of the Fire clans, sitting in a fork of the tree, gazing towards the town of Winston. Although he was the oldest and wisest of the Faeries, Ashreyel still longed to find a companion with whom his spiritual essence could be intertwined, and now, as he spied the slim form of Dyllenae Kindleblaze, his heart leapt in his chest with the first glow of love's sparks.

Saying nothing, he watched her from a distance, his heart moved by the fire in her eyes, the flash of her smile. However, the longer he observed her, the more troubled he became. He saw that her eyes, while flashing with fire and beauty, tended towards scorn as she watched the women from the village about their chores. Often he noticed her gazing at her reflection in a stream or pool, entranced by her own loveliness. Eventually he could no longer deny the fact that the one on whom his heart had fixed was cursed with pride.

He beseeched her to change her ways and to embrace humility, but she would not listen, and Ashreyel grew angry. However, his love meant that he desired the best for her, and so he performed a terrible spell. When next a woman from the village came to the forest to gather herbs, and Dyllenae Kindleblaze looked with contempt upon her human ugliness, her clumsiness, her mortality, Ashreyel sent the Faerie into a deep sleep. Then he took her spirit and placed it in the woman, there to dwell, a silent observer of the woman's life, until the day the mortal died, whereupon the spell would be broken. Ashreyel's heart was heavy at the thought of his love leading the life of a mortal, experiencing pain and heartache, yet he hardened his resolve and swore to remain near to Dyllenae for the years of the mortal woman's life.

As time passed, Dyllenae observed the young woman grow to maturity. She felt the woman's nervous pangs when she fell in love She experienced the ecstasy of love first consummated, the tender joy of the mother holding in her arms her first child. Dyllenae became observer to many emotions, to love and hate, joy and fear, sorrow and the pain of deep loss. Through the woman's eyes she saw a reflection that grew older with time, wrinkles forming at the corners of her eyes, strands of grey masking the rich chestnut of her hair. At the end of the woman's life, as her husband held her close and whispered words of love, Dyllenae Kindleblaze finally realized what it meant to be human.

At that moment, in the hushed and darkened room of a mean cottage, where a mortal man she had come to know and admire knelt at the bedside of the wife he had loved so desperately, Dyllenae became aware of a song filtering through the shuttered windows. It was a song of haunting power, sung in a mellifluous voice, the song of Ashreyel calling her back to him. As she listened, Dyllenae Kindleblaze's heart mourned, and she regretted her years of despising those less fortunate than herself. She vowed that in future she would strive to fulfil

the purpose for which she was created; she would nurture and protect, and have compassion for mortal beings.

In that instant her spirit lifted, and she awoke, her lovely features glowing with radiance. Her understanding of the true virtues in life made her more beautiful than ever before. By her side was the faithful Ashreyel, who had guided her into new responsibility. He was overjoyed: at last he had found the true reflection of his being, one who shared his innermost desires and dreams. So it was that their spirits intertwined, and in their communion they were inseparable.

As Alarissa finished the tale of Dyllenae Kindleblaze, she smiled. I forced myself to bite my tongue and reflected on what I had heard. If the Faerie are so closely allied to their mortal kin, what then of the similarities between Man and other animals? If Man can resemble the Faerie in some ways, is it not possible that the lower animals could resemble ourselves? I dwelled on this thought as I made my way home.

overleaf: Dyllenae Kindleblaze

Tuesday, 28th October 1664

'It was at this very spot that the hunt in Winston Forest was forever vanquished,' said Alarissa as we made our way down a path through the tall trees, a trail I was sure I had never encountered before. We had decided to take our lessons to the forest, and our walk was punctuated by the sharp crack of twigs and rustle of fallen leaves. Alarissa Fernspray's delicate tread roused not one snap or whisper from the forest floor.

Some time ago I had heard that the local hunt had disbanded, and had thought it strange at the time, for there is nothing a man likes better of an evening than boasting to his friends over a tankard of ale of a successful day's hunting. As I turned to ask Alarissa about this occurrence, my appetite for learning was so obvious in my face that she laughed delightedly.

'Truly, you are an excellent student!' she said, smiling radiantly. 'This is what occurred that fateful day,' she continued, and settled herself to relate her tale.

Ethereal Abandon

The Tale of Caerlena Fenmire and the Winston Hunt

A young fox was making his way through the forest in the early morning light when the sounds a fox dreads came drifting to him on the breeze. It was the belling of hounds in full cry, their howls and baying leaving the fox in little doubt as to their intent. He picked up his pace and was soon racing through the forest, unheeding of the branches that blocked his path, caring for nothing but the need to get back to his earth where his cubs and vixen awaited him. He attempted all the tricks at his disposal to throw the hounds off his scent, running through streams that crossed his path, leaping onto high logs and frisking neatly along their length before jumping to the ground again. But the cries of the hounds came ever closer.

Eventually, racked with exhaustion and his sides heaving with panic, he stopped in a clearing. He knew he must not lead the hunt to where his mate and cubs lay curled together, and so he chose rather to make his stand. He turned to face the oncoming hounds. It was a matter of moments before the pack raced in. The hooves of the horses and the cries of the men echoed from the trees around the clearing. The fox bared his teeth and flattened his ears, preparing to sell his life as dearly as he could for the sake of his family.

At this moment, as fox and hounds faced each other across the leaf-littered forest floor, Caerlena Fenmire stepped in.

As an Earth Faerie, it was her duty to care for the creatures of the forest, guarding them from harm. From a distance she had heard the commotion of the hunt as it made its discordant way through the peace of the forest, and had hurried to see what might be done.

Comprised as they are of spirit, Faeries are not usually visible to mortal eyes. However, they are often readily apparent to animals, since these are more in touch with their spiritual natures than are humans. So it was that both fox and hounds gradually became aware of the presence of the Faerie, and a hush fell on the scene. Gracefully she stepped between them, her hands held out placatingly.

'Look at yourselves,' she chided gently. 'You are brothers from ages past. Your birth lines stem from the same source. Yet you face each other with a hatred that exists not of your own choosing, but which is placed in your hearts by the desires of Man.' The dogs eyed each other uncomfortably, and the fox pricked up his ears. As she felt the tension dissipating, Caerlena addressed the hounds. 'If Man had not inspired you to attack, had not trained you from puppyhood to desire the death of other creatures, would you be here now? Would you choose the death of your brother over the displeasure of your human masters? Your desire should be for the prospering of each species, not its decimation.'

Turning to the fox, who was now basking lazily with a self-satisfied expression on his face, Caerlena Fenmire raised a hand to pluck a small white chicken feather from his snout, a remnant of his ill-gotten morning meal. 'And you, Master Fox, should not engender the dislike of your brothers by stealing from them that which it is their duty to protect. Take your prey in the forest, as nature ordains, rather than by sneaky, unscrupulous means in the chicken coops of Man. For your own behaviour has drawn the hunt to you this day; the choices you have made are responsible for your downfall.'

At that moment the horses, bearing their human masters, thundered into the clearing. With a whisk of his tail, the fox turned and disappeared into the undergrowth, his lesson well-learned. The horses, seeing the Faerie, halted abruptly, their breath steaming in the chill air.

The riders urged their mounts forward, but to no avail. Quietly Caerlena walked towards the horses, and although they rolled their eyes and baulked at her presence, they made no move to escape her.

Nature Conservation

'Truly,' she said to them, 'all animals are brothers. The stag you chase with abandon through the forest, at the command of your masters, is your comrade. Respect him, and let the preservation of his life be your highest goal.' With this she placed a gentle hand on each noble brow, and their wild eyes quietened, taking on a look of pride.

The men, more uneasy with each moment's passing, were unnerved by the strange silence and perhaps even glimpsed a shadowy figure. One by one each remembered chores that had been left undone and, calling their hounds to heel, they turned the horses for home.

There never was another hunt in Winston Forest. The men found that their mounts baulked and refused the saddle, or developed lameness within the first few paces on the trail. The hounds failed to find a scent, or ran and gambolled in the fields like puppies before falling down to sleep in the shade of the trees, and no command from their human masters could bring them to heel. The men soon realised that any hunt would have to be on foot or not at all.

And unaccountably, chicken coops were no longer raided by hungry foxes, even in the depths of winter. Men simply dismissed it as coincidence, but how many such happenings can be attributed to the intervention of the Faerie?

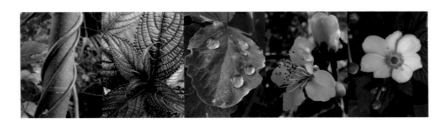

I had not seen Alarissa the previous day, but today she greeted me in the usual manner, launching herself into another story. I always take a scrap of paper and a quill and ink with me to the pool now, to scribble down her complex tales. Now, in the evening, I try to make sense of my scrawls, as I sit close to the fire with my cat Mog on my lap. This is the tale Alarissa told me today.

The Great Deed of Bayarde Nutbrown

Ashreyel, who had come to be known as Ashreyel the Wise, made many sojourns amongst the clans of Faerie. After the fall of so many of their number, he was keen to observe the clans, at times in secret, in order to prevent the dissipation of the entire Faerie race.

He had made his home in Winston Forest, where the ancient tree Wisewood stood. Ashreyel drew great comfort and inspiration from the tree and often stopped there to ponder the ways of the world.

He was in his favourite place one day when a small group of Faerie clansfolk made their way past the tree. They were deep in discussion, and he remained quiet so as not to alert them to his presence. They were discussing who amongst them was able to perform the greatest feats, as youngsters everywhere are apt to do. Ashreyel settled himself at the bole of the tree, secretly amused.

'It is clear that Faeries of the Fire clans have the most might,' Eliyada Smokewisp, a guardian of Fire, said boldly. He stood confidently in the middle of the group. 'All here remember the lightning blast that struck the Lookout Tree and blazed through the surrounding countryside in a wall of bright fire.' He paused for effect. 'It was I who prevented the devastation such a fire would have caused and saved the whole forest. Fire has the greatest

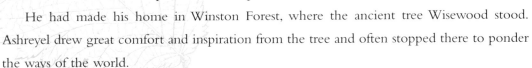

Dorran Spindrift

Eliyada Smokewisp

power for destruction, yet when it is tamed it gives light and heat and is Man's most useful tool. Thus Fire should hold the place of the greatest amongst us.' His cinder-wings swept the air around him, and he looked just and noble.

The other Faeries were clearly impressed. However, the guardian of one of the Water clans, Dorran Spindrift, made a show of examining his perfect nails.

'That is very impressive, I am sure,' he drawled in bored tones. 'I believe otherwise, however.' He quelled Eliyada Smokewisp's protests with a nonchalant wave of his hand and continued. 'Not long ago, a terrible flood threatened the entire town of Winston when the river overflowed its banks. It was I who single-handedly averted the disaster. Water, too, has great power for destruction and yet it brings life and abundance to all around. But tell me, what use would Fire be if Water quelled its might? If Fire is powerful, it is clear that Water is more so, and thus is the greatest of the elements.'

At this a heated discussion broke out amongst the group, and the elegant Baydonn Cloudweaver stepped forward. His massive wings, richly feathered as those of the birds, stirred up a great draught until the Faeries fell silent.

Baydonn Cloudweaver

'What Fire and Water have claimed is true,' he began, and the two Faeries nodded eagerly in agreement. 'Both have immense power for good or ruin. But consider Air,' he continued, glaring at Eliyada Smokewisp. 'None can survive without the benefit of the air as breath. The wind brings the clouds which cause the rain to fall and the lightning to flash. The drought of many years was broken when I caused the wind to sweep the clouds from the sea over the land. Both fire and water are at the mercy of the wind. It can blow them where it will, and they must obey. Air can dry up water and extinguish fire. Therefore Air is the mightiest of the elements.'

The other Faeries conceded the truth of his words. Ashreyel shook his head wryly and would have moved on had his attention not been caught by the change in tone of the discussion.

'We have heard impressive tales of the greatness of the clans,' pronounced Eliyada Smokewisp. 'But there is one amongst us who has said nothing at all.' He turned to the Earth Faerie, Bayarde Nutbrown, who stood silent. 'What have you to say, Nutbrown?' Eliyada asked him. 'Is there nothing you have done to match our achievements? No deeds, noble and true, that you can relate to burnish the reputation of your clan?'

The other Faeries glanced at one another in amusement, for the Earth Faeries were widely considered to be the most humble and lowly of the clans.

Nutbrown spoke. 'You are correct, Eliyada Smokewisp, to assume that I have performed no great feats of might or magic. My time has been dedicated to planting and cultivating, and to protecting the small creatures from harm.' He looked down unassumingly.

'But there must be something,' said Dorran Spindrift in amazement. 'An action that was out of the ordinary in any way? A noble deed? Anything?' he asked hopefully, for he was fond of Bayarde Nutbrown and would not see him humiliated in front of the other Faeries.

Bayarde replied slowly. 'I have rescued a small child who was lost in the forest, and seen him safely back to his mother. Without my intervention he would surely have died, for it was winter and bitterly cold.'

There was a moment of stunned silence, before hilarity broke out. 'That is your great deed?' laughed Eliyada Smokewisp. 'It is better than I had hoped,' he cried, wiping tears of laughter from his eyes.

Nutbrown said nothing, burning with embarrassment. The other three, having had their amusement at his expense, returned to their argument.

Bayarde Nutbrown

It was then that Ashreyel the Wise chose to intervene. He appeared suddenly, his face fierce, and the four Faeries were thrown abruptly into confusion, bowing low before him.

Eliyada Smokewisp found the courage to speak first. 'We meant no harm, Ashreyel the Wise. It was clear that the deeds we have performed are so much greater than those of the Earth Faeries, and we were amused.'

Ashreyel did not reply for what seemed like an age. Eventually he spoke. 'Which of you would even exist without the maintaining force of Earth?' he demanded. 'Without Earth what would you burn, Fire? What would you nourish, Water? On what would you blow, Air?' He paused and looked around before continuing. 'But life demands more than that. Each living creature has its origins in the dust of the earth. It breathes of the air and nourishes itself with the water and the produce of the earth. It is warmed and given light by the sun's fire.'

Stooping down, Ashreyel picked up a pine cone. He placed it in the palm of his hand and held it out to them. In the other hand, a fire began to glow. The Faeries watched, spellbound. Slowly Ashreyel brought his hands together. As the first rays of the fire's heat smote it, the tightly closed cone began to open, unfolding gradually like the petals of a flower, to reveal the precious seeds buried deep within. 'This is the spark of new life,' Ashreyel said, 'but it is only potential at present.' With a wave of his hand the fire disappeared.

Now Ashreyel began to blow gently on the pine cone. A mild wind sprang up, and the seeds were whipped from the pine cone to dance in the breeze, before coming to rest gently on the ground. At the touch of the earth, the seeds embedded themselves rapidly. Ashreyel stretched out his staff and a light rain began to fall, soaking into the soil and nourishing the dormant seeds. 'Grow,' he commanded softly, and the amazed Faeries watched as small shoots began to push their way blindly towards the heat and fire of the sun, drawing sustenance from the earth that nourished them, the water that dampened them, and the cool breeze that blew through their tiny leaves.

'The cycle of new life is unending, and if any element is absent, a new tree will not grow,' Ashreyel explained. The chastened Faeries glanced at one another sheepishly. 'Go,' commanded Ashreyel, 'and avoid such foolishness in future. Faeries of the different elements should labour together without resentment, each prepared to accord to the others the work that they do best.'

The Faeries made their way from the clearing. Only Baydonn Cloudweaver lingered.

'All you have said is true,' said the Wind Faerie, turning back to Ashreyel even as he waved his friends to go on without him. 'But I would ask one question of you.'

'Ask, then,' answered Ashreyel.

Baydonn twitched his wings in discomfort. 'All the clans have performed awesome feats. They have averted disasters of fire and water and drought. Yet the Earth Faerie has merely saved a child from death. What is one child compared to the many we have saved in the course of our actions?'

Ashreyel considered his words. 'Can you see into the future?' he asked. The Faerie looked at him in bemusement before shaking his head. 'Can you tell what it is this child will become when he is grown? What if I were to remind you that this child has the potential for greatness buried inside him? That one day he will be a leader of men such as has never before been seen on the earth. Does that change your view of the Earth Faerie's actions?'

'It makes sense to rescue such a one,' Baydonn admitted.

'What if I were to reveal that in the future there is potential for the same child to use his power for evil, bringing destruction and terror to all? What then would be your view?'

The Wind Faerie thought for some time before asking, 'Would it not be better to let him perish in the forest, rather than bringing devastation to the worlds of Man and Faerie?'

Ashreyel shook his head sadly. 'The paths of the future are many. Along some, that child may go on to achieve much that is good and just, and thereby improve the world. Others may lead to death and ruin. Regardless of which future he chooses, you and I have no right to remove that choice from him. The paths were laid out by the hand of the Supreme Source and Maker of All Life before the child's creation, and we cannot interfere. We may have created either a saviour or a destroyer, but either way, we cannot change our actions.'

After a moment's silence Ashreyel continued. 'Every deed, no matter how small, has an impact on the paths of the future. Therefore you should strive to direct those paths towards good, and not evil. Who knows, perhaps young Bayarde Nutbrown, with his simple act of kindness towards a lost and frightened child, has placed that child on the path to virtue.' Ashreyel gazed fiercely at Baydonn Cloudweaver, but there was a twinkle in his eyes. 'Go now,' he told him, 'and join your friends. All are equal in the sight of the Supreme Source and Maker of All Life.'

'What is the lesson for this day?' I asked as I arrived at the pool.

Alarissa looked thoughtful. She caught a wisp of feather from a branch, where it was snagged, before replying. 'I will tell you more of the Guardians of the Faeries.' She blew the feather gently into the air where it drifted on the currents of the breeze, then settled herself comfortably and began.

The Air Faeries

Air is the very breath of life, without which nothing can have its being. Air Faeries are as light as gossamer, as delicate as soap bubbles, hardly needing the magnificent wings that sprout from their shoulders to achieve their buoyant flight. It is their delight to care for the birds, animals and plants of the air, escorting dandelion seeds borne on the wind to the best places for them to grow, and gently guiding the swallows in their migrations.

overleaf: Jaide Leafwhirl

Amburr Sunsparkle

Jaide Leafwhirl's clan revels in the gusts of wind that pick up the fallen autumn leaves and whirl them into the air in a shower of gold and red. They are enraptured by the scent of spring petals tossed on the breeze, enthralled by the musty leaves and sun-ripened fruits shaken from the trees. In the rattle of bare branches in the midst of winter's chill, in the rustle of green shoots and new-formed leaves, they relish the freedom of the wind, ever restless and invigorating, whipping seeds from pods into sweeping flight.

The gentle breeze that cools the hot summer days is the responsibility of Amburr

Sheonnia Wildwind

Sunsparkle's clan. Theirs is the clan of burnished sunlight filtering through fluttering green leaves, casting spangled patterns on the earth, of gusts of warm air that liven a frozen winter scene. To them belong the smells of sun-warmed earth and baked leaves, the drone of drowsy bees and the dance of nectar-sated butterflies.

The rough winds that blow icily across the frozen landscape and drive the rain-gorged clouds are the domain of Sheonnia Wildwind's clan. With fierce joy they whip the branches of the trees and dash the icy daggers of rain and snow against the hard earth. Theirs is the heady rush of air that brings colour to the cheeks and tears to the eyes, the scents of sea and brine smelled far inland.

Endowed with mighty wings, Baydonn Cloudweaver's clan combs the clouds into fleecy tails that trail across the skies. Their domain is that of refreshing summer rain that brings relief from stifling heat. Their realm is embellished by the intricate patterns woven by the wind into the clouds, ripples and eddies, swirls and spirals. Enthroned in the heights of the heavens, thunderheads and cumulus clouds billow up at their breath, and the Faeries' untamed joy is seen in the flashes of lightning that streak across the lowering sky.

Monday, 3rd November 1664

The winter winds grow more bitter, and many nights I awake with my throat constricted and barely enough breath in my body to keep me alive. I have lived the full three score and ten years allotted to me, so I do not fear leaving this world, yet I wonder how my passing will affect Alarissa Fernspray.

I tentatively broached the subject with her this morning as we sat in the weak sunlight filtering down to the Pool of Half-Remembered Dreams.

'I am afraid that I may soon leave you, Alarissa,' I began hesitantly.

She looked up from the dry leaf she was examining. 'Leave?' she queried. 'Are you to undertake a journey?'

'Of a sort,' I replied, at a loss. I tried again. 'I feel as though my time on this earth is drawing to a close. The winter of my life is come, and the sleep of death awaits me.'

'The winter of your life?' she repeated, with a trill of laughter like the song of a bird. 'Truly, you mortals have some strange concepts!'

I was vexed by her lack of seriousness, and answered her brusquely. 'It is an expression we humans use to describe the season when all has withered and died and nothing is left but death.'

She appeared greatly distressed by my words. 'What a sad and lonely thought,' she eventually concluded. 'We Faerie have a different view, for although we are not mortal, we are not impervious to what it means to have a finite number of days on the earth.' She picked up a small seed and began to explain.

'Winter is seen by the Faerie as a time of birth, a season of great potential. Under the blanketing snows, the seeds lie waiting for the first rays of the sun, which will bring them into germination and so to fruition.' She held out the seed to me. 'Trees conserve energy for the burst of flowering that spring will require. Animals sleep, cosy in their burrows, knowing that with spring will come a time of mating, when their species will be renewed. The world stands on the brink of the new and exciting season of rebirth. The Faerie see this as the age of childhood. The human child is merely a seed, dormant yet full of potential.'

She closed her fingers gently around the seed. When she opened her hand, it had split its

Baydonn Cloudweaver

shiny skin and put forth a small root and a shoot of verdant green that sought the light. 'Spring and early summer are the seasons of great blossoming,' she continued, 'when the leaves appear on the trees and the earth is made beautiful by flowers and fragranced with the scent of herbs. The rich loam of the forest encourages the plants to grow tall and sturdy, to achieve the potential within each of them. Animals are creating a generation of new young to populate the earth. In the springtime of a man's life, he acquires knowledge and experience, fulfilling the promise of greatness that has lain dormant within.' As she spoke, the shoot put forth leaves and flowers, blossoming to form a tiny, perfect tree. As I watched, the flowers blew away to leave the beginnings of fruit, tiny and delicate, amongst the leaves.

'By late summer, all growth is done. The fruits have ripened on the trees until they are full of mellow sweetness. The animals have raised their young, who are ready to attempt lives of their own. It is a season of achievement, rich with the savour of hard work completed. Nothing more is left to be done but to appreciate the fruits of the labours one has faithfully carried out. Man is at his full potential, bearing fruit and enriching his own life and those of others with his experience and knowledge.

'With autumn comes the harvest. The abundant growth of a year of potential, toil and fulfilment is gathered home. This is the season the Faerie see as death. Not a heartless slaying by a bitter wind and cruel snows, or a freezing sleep of oblivion; merely the gentle gathering in of a harvest to be used to enrich the lives of future generations.'

Her voice trailed away and gradually the vision of the fragile tree faded until there was nothing in her palm but a seed.

My eyes were filled with tears. 'Alarissa,' I said finally, 'our times together have been precious to me, more so than I can express. I have learned many things about your race, and even more about my own. Yet nothing you have ever said has meant more to me than this.'

As I left her that day, I tried to think of my life as a tree. How would the Supreme Source view me when it came time for my harvest to be gathered? Would my life be filled with love and happiness? Or would I be a twisted stump, absorbing the nutrients of the abundant earth yet keeping all for myself? I pray to God that I would be the sort of tree that animals and birds would choose for their home!

Jaide Leafwhirl and Raelle Lavenderbalm

Friday, 7th November 1664

Yet again the harsh winds and driving rain confine me to my cottage. I yearn to be with Alarissa – I realize that my times with her offer an escape from loneliness, though I should be used to solitude by now.

I think back to the day I first met my love, Jonathan. My life up to this point had been filled with turmoil, and I had run away to find peace in a place many miles from my home town. I had found work as a dairymaid, a far cry from my previous existence. If my family could have seen me then, how shocked they would have been, and the fine husband they had chosen for me would have turned up his nose at the stench of the cows.

I was a dark-haired, dark-eyed lass of eighteen, far too outspoken and impetuous for a gentlewoman, and I assumed my new role with gusto. However, I was suspicious of anyone who tried to befriend me, for I was fearful they would discover my secret. Thus I kept others at arm's length, and although in this I found a measure of security, I had thereby also embraced a deep and enduring loneliness.

When first I met Jonathan, I was making my way back in the purple light of the evening to the farm where I had my lodgings. The fragrance of elderflowers was heavy in the air, and the joyously returning swallows decorated the violet sky. In a field next to the track was a maypole, ready for the welcoming of May, and through the dusk I caught sight of a tall stranger standing beneath it, gazing into the sky. It was a scene of arresting beauty, and without making a sound I crept towards the stranger until I was close behind him.

'The conversation one can have with a maypole must be rather limited,' I joked loudly,

expecting him to jump in alarm at my voice. He did not move, however, merely continued to stare up at the gaudily painted pole.

'Oh, I don't know,' he mused, almost as though to himself. 'It tells of joy and love, of secrets and dances, of springs past and springs future. It speaks to us of hope, of the winter passing and the return of summer to the land.'

For a moment I was speechless. He turned to face me, and the starlight caught the pale glint of his eyes. It was as though they were made of quicksilver, with almost no colour to them, and in confusion, I turned away from him. 'You are not from these parts, obviously,' I eventually muttered, feeling like an idiot.

'No, I am not,' he replied gravely. He made me feel like a gauche and graceless girl again. 'I am from London.'

'Very grand, I am sure,' I said to him, acting like the peasant he apparently took me to be. He made no reply, staring at me with those unfathomable eyes until I grew uncomfortable. It felt as though he had seen into the depths of my soul with a single glance, and it made me angry. I decided that retreat was the only dignity left to me now. 'Forgive me for disturbing you, your highness,' I remarked sarcastically as I walked away.

He let me go a few paces before reaching out and capturing my hand in his long, elegant fingers. 'Wait, don't go,' he whispered. 'To part from you is to die a little.'

'I do not care to stay,' I replied.

I disentangled my hand and flounced from the field, half hoping that he would call me back. But he did not. When I risked a glance back at him, he was in the same position as when I had first seen him, staring up at the fluttering ribbons on the pole.

In the excitement of the preparations for May Day the stranger was soon out of my mind. That year I was crowned the Queen of the May, and the villagers said they had not seen a more lovely queen in many a season. But on my triumphant day, there was the stranger, smiling

at me from the surging crowd. He gazed at me with an intensity that was frightening and thrilling at the same time.

I opened the festivities with the first of the dances around the maypole. A team of dancers accompanied me, and we started the dance with exuberant high spirits and laughter. Yet it was quickly clear that the pattern was not weaving itself as it should have. The ribbons were full of snarls and tangles, and as I moved round the pole I saw a tall youth, dancing with abandon ever closer to me. His face was not visible under the brim of his hat, and as he drew level with me, he swept me into his arms, twirling us around in the white ribbon until we were hopelessly entangled. The crowd roared with laughter as the dance came to an inglorious end.

At once I recognized the face of the stranger, his cool eyes intent on mine. He was grinning, and if I had not been so angry, I would have felt my knees weaken. 'Put me down, you lout,' I objected loudly, frightened at the feelings aroused by his nearness. I struggled in his arms until the ribbon around us pulled tight and we crashed heavily to the ground. The crowd tittered.

'I swear to you,' he whispered as we lay together under the shadow of the maypole, 'I will never let you go again, my beauty.'

The sincerity in his voice cut through the embarrassment I was feeling, and spoke eloquently to the part of me that needed to be held and loved. So it was that I met his gaze, and for the first time I smiled at him, uncertainly, until the moment was broken and the onlookers demanded their turn in the dance.

We were soon untangled and the stranger silently grasped my hand in his and led me, unresisting, to where the forest meets the stream. There he spread his threadbare jacket, and as the joyous noise of the festivities rose behind us, we sat and talked of things that were important to us, of life and love and times past and future. Perhaps, as he had gazed at that maypole the first night of our meeting, he had seen a glimpse of our time together, so achingly short, and it had spurred his capture of me. Now it is too late to ask, for Jonathan Shawe is gone from me, and all that is left is the heap of stones that I gathered to mark his grave in the meadow where we met.

Raelle Lavenderbalm and Dorran Spindrift

Monday, 10th November 1664

Today I paid a visit to Dame Kemp's house, to take a remedy to her young son. As I approached their ramshackle cottage, I noticed the eldest child, a girl, standing in the garden near the wishing well. As she turned her beautiful but vacant gaze towards me I remembered her inability to speak normally, her slowness to learn, and her strange, childish gait, even though she was fourteen. She smiled at me radiantly, before shambling closer and putting her hand gently on my arm. She gazed up earnestly, then suddenly lost interest and wandered off.

Shaking my head with pity, I made my way to the hut and was ushered into its shabby interior by Dame Kemp. While examining her painfully thin son, I glanced out of the window and noticed a curious display. The girl was looking into the depths of the well and conversing earnestly with something I could not perceive. I could hear snatches of incomprehensible babble, and at times she

Bryar Nutbrown

Huntar Nutbrown

would laugh delightedly and wave her hands in the air as though encouraging others in a dance.

Dame Kemp made her way to the window and looked out.

'Aye, away with the Faeries, that one is,' she commented sadly, before turning back to her son.

When I had finished attending to the boy I took my leave. My way home led me past the Pool of Half-Remembered Dreams, more by design than by chance, for I felt I needed Alarissa Fernspray's wisdom to make sense of what I had seen. When I described the girl, Alarissa was at first confused.

'I know not of whom you speak,' she said blithely, and shrugged her lovely shoulders, clad in their garment of mist-fine leaves.

'She is the simpleton who lives with her family close to the old wishing well, the blonde child who can neither speak like a normal person nor communicate with others.'

'Simpleton?' queried Alarissa, as though the same malady had struck her too.

'Halfwit, dullard, one of lesser intelligence,' I continued, exasperated. She stared at me blankly for a few moments, then comprehension dawned.

'I think you refer to Tiltann,' she said eventually, with a rueful smile on her face.

Fleur Lavenderbalm

'No, you are mistaken – the child's name is Mary.'

'Tiltann in the language of the Faerie refers to a clover blossom. Have you ever looked at a flower like that?' she questioned, and when I shrugged in affirmation, she shook her head. 'Have you gazed into its complexities, at the beauty of its tiny stamens, the frill of its delicate petals? It grows everywhere, easy to trample, seemingly insignificant, yet the honey produced from it is deemed among the sweetest known.

'So it is with the child you call Mary. Although she is seen by many as unimportant, a mindless creature to be pitied or ignored, Faeries are drawn to her indomitable spirit, her innocence, and her joy in life. We regularly converse with her, and to us she makes perfect sense. In fact, you probably witnessed such a discourse today, for the Faeries love to go to the wishing well and dance for Tiltann there.'

I felt suitably chastened, and could not meet Alarissa's eyes as I asked the next question. 'Why could I not see the Faeries that danced for her? I see you without effort.'

Alarissa smiled. 'The simplest of all concepts confound the wise,' she uttered. 'It is only when you look with the heart of a child, artless and untroubled by the hardships of life, that you truly see that which is invisible to the physical eye.'

As I write, I ponder the irony that the child for whom I have felt pity for so long perhaps should pity me.

Friday, 14th November 1664

At present I sit by the fire, deciphering the notes I have made from my visits to Alarissa over the past four days. The weather has been mild of late and so I have visited her as often as I could. But on returning home, I have been too weary to set pen to paper. So on this chilly, wet night, I am resigning myself to hard work by the fireside.

Ashreyel the Wise and Daecien Darkmist

In the days before the Great Falling Away of the Faerie, Ashreyel the Wise was no different from the other Faeries. Like them, he wandered the earth, searching for acts of depredation and destruction committed by Man and setting them to rights. In all these journeys, his closest companion was a Faerie by the name of Daecien Darkmist. The two Faeries, though inseparable, were by their very nature opposites, yet this served only to strengthen their bond of companionship and mutual respect. Where Ashreyel was calm and measured, deliberate in all his actions, Daecien was fiery and wild, impulsive and quick to act.

For many years the two Faeries travelled together. Both took the commands of the Supreme Source and Maker of All Life to heart, and in their actions they laboured to lead Man back to him. Yet as time passed, Ashreyel noticed that Daecien was growing more distant and reserved. When Ashreyel asked him what was troubling him, however, Daecien flashed him a smile and denied that anything was wrong.

One day, as they were strolling together through a forest, they came upon a starving dog and her litter of pups. The hound was so thin her ribs stuck out through her mangy coat, yet she showed a feverish resolve to survive for the sake of her puppies. From the welts on her hide it was clear she had received many beatings, and her eyes reflected the patient resignation of an animal long used to mistreatment. She lay curled protectively around her four blind pups, and as the Faeries approached, her tail thumped the ground in welcome. Gently Daecien knelt and placed a tender hand upon the dog's faithful head, and a hardness came into his eyes as he looked up at Ashreyel.

'This is one who has offered her love to another and has had it scorned. She would have given her very life for her master. She kept the rats from his grain and helped him herd the animals of his fields. She even saved his child from death when it fell into a stream.' His hands smoothed the shaggy fur. 'Yet this is her reward,' he continued. 'Beaten every day of her existence, starved and made to search for her own food, and when she was pregnant with pups, tied up and left to die.' Ashreyel put his hand on his comrade's shoulder in silent understanding, but Daecien shrugged it off impatiently. 'How can we make excuses for such a one?' he asked. 'How long will Man continue with his cruel whims and insane desires?'

Delicately Daecien picked up each of the squirming, hungry puppies, then motioned for the mother to follow him. He led her through the forest to where an old blind man lived by himself in a ramshackle cottage, then placed the puppies carefully at the door and knocked twice before disappearing. The two Faeries watched as the old man opened the door. The mangy dog butted against his legs with her head, and absently he bent down to pat her.

'What have we here?' he mumbled to himself as one of the pups squalled in hunger. With searching hands he located each of the puppies and carried them inside as the mother dog watched anxiously. As Ashreyel and Daecien departed, she was licking clean a large bowl of milk the old man had placed on the floor for her.

'My heart is indeed heavy, my friend,' Daecien admitted to Ashreyel when they had journeyed some distance. 'When such a faithful dog gives her life to serve a master who is not worthy, I question the rightness of the world.' Ashreyel made as though to speak, but Daecien held up his hand. 'Nay, Mirror of my Being,' he said. 'Do not seek to persuade me otherwise. In our travels I have seen much cruelty and pain. It builds up in my spirit like a monstrous growth that devours the healthy flesh, and I fear it will take my very life.'

'The Supreme Source and Maker of All Life has created us to protect and nurture,' said Ashreyel, 'and it is his will that we do so.'

'Why should we nurture what others have destroyed? What gives Man the right to inflict

cruelty, devastation and pain? He was designed to be the Crown of Creation, yet he has made himself unworthy to be even the lowest of the animals.'

'The Supreme Source has willed it so that Man has a right to choose between the evil in his nature and the good. We cannot decide for him,' said Ashreyel.

To this Daecien could say nothing, though his heart was heavy. He knew his friend spoke the truth, yet implicit in that truth was a reproach of Daecien's own feelings and desires. In his mind, his friend's face grew dim and unfocused, as though he glimpsed him from far away, and Daecien shivered.

86

Sylvan Frolics

It seemed that Daecien was not alone in his feelings. At the Council of the Faeries that took place soon after this incident, the Impostor put forward his plan to remove man from the world and replace him with the Faeries. In one fell swoop, Daecien Darkmist felt all of his fears and torments understood and condoned. As the Impostor beguiled Faeries with his words of power, Daecien was flushed with excitement, his eyes glowing with a fervour that had once been engendered only by the performance of good deeds. With a single searching look in Ashreyel's direction, he questioned all that the other Faerie held to be true, and he knew from Ashreyel's answering glance that his friend would never deny his beliefs.

A sense of betrayal flooded Daecien Darkmist then, for he knew that Ashreyel harboured the same doubts as he did, yet the other Faerie had remained unmoved by the words of the stranger. As the Impostor left the gathering, Daecien followed in his wake, his deep hurt and anger at Ashreyel sitting like a cold stone in his breast, mingling with the sour taste of his own guilt and shame.

The Conflict Begins

The Impostor and the multitude of Faeries he had swayed with his arguments took up their dwellings in the dark places of the earth. In the slimy caverns and cold places under the mountains, in the depths of the most gloomy forests they had their abode. At the instigation of the Impostor, these Faeries began to distort and twist the nature that had been so perfectly created by the Supreme Source of All Life. Plants and trees that had once flowered into fruitful loveliness grew small and mean, and the dank and dismal caves and dripping woodlands became rife with diseased fungus and lichen. The followers of the Impostor adopted a new name for themselves – from this time forward they would be known as the Faeries of Chaos, for through their efforts they hoped to provoke confusion and dismay on the earth.

The Impostor was cunning, and over time the Chaos Faeries came to believe and wholeheartedly support his notion of a world where Man no longer dwelt. Even Daecien Darkmist upheld the Impostor's lies, for his heart was hardened by the cruelties that he had witnessed in such abundance. The Impostor spent much time with Daecien, placing doubts in his mind about his friendship with Ashreyel and the futility of the latter's cause. 'Is it not possible,' he whispered on countless occasions, 'that Ashreyel, the one they call the Wise, used you to accomplish his purposes? For oft have you told me of plans that were his, yet the pursuance of them belonged to you alone.'

At first Daecien listened unwillingly to these words, for he could not forget so soon the companionship of Ashreyel and all it had meant to him. But over time his heart became ever more angry and hardened against the Faerie, and especially hostile to Ashreyel, who had remained unwavering in his calling. Daecien Darkmist took joy in his persecution of Man, remembering all the animals left to die in cruel traps, the forests raped for wood for Man's fires, the rivers floating with effluent and the skies darkened with smoke. Every blow he struck was a blow to Ashreyel's heart, and Daecien rejoiced in the feelings of power and vengeance.

As the years passed, Daecien Darkmist became the Faerie closest to the Impostor, privy to his most warped ideas and darkest secrets. At the same time, the Faeries of Chaos grew more zealous in their actions against the tyranny of Man, setting his barns on fire, destroying his crops with blight and his animals with plague. In his frustration Man attacked his fellows, causing hatred and mayhem amongst the peoples of earth. The Faeries of Chaos mimicked Ashreyel's ideas, forming clans to control the various elements. The wicked earth clans caused famine to scourge the lands. The Chaos Faeries of the air induced great storms to blow, causing terrible destruction. Creation was ravaged by fire and floods and laid desolate by drought. In the midst of the turmoil, Man turned accusing eyes on the heavens, shaking his fist at the Supreme Source and Maker of All Life. And the Impostor laughed at his own triumph.

Those who had remained faithful to Ashreyel and the cause were dismayed by the power of the evil that surrounded them. They tried with all their might to limit the destruction and havoc caused by the Faeries of Chaos, but to no avail, for they were scattered all over the world.

'What can we do?' they asked Ashreyel repeatedly, and each time he replied, 'If we take up the cause of Man against the Faeries of Chaos, we become like them. How shall we be distinguished from the evil and destruction?'

The Faeries were silenced by his wisdom, yet in his heart of hearts Ashreyel remained torn. He called a gathering of the Guardians of the clans to decide what should be done. It was a sombre group that met in the shade of Wisewood. Each Faerie came with a story of terrible destruction or havoc, and their sadness at the betrayal of so many of their kind was evident in their weary eyes.

'Friends,' said Ashreyel, when they had all gathered round, 'we are faced with a terrible choice. Our lives and those of Man are interlinked, as the Supreme Source and Maker of All Life intended from the creation of the world. Therefore, what disturbs Man must also concern the Faerie.' He looked around at their faces, each bearing the strain of the uncertainty they were confronting. 'We are besieged by the Faeries of Chaos on every side, and their might grows as each day passes. Man blames the one who made him for the trials he faces, and the Faeries of Chaos encourage him to fall ever further from the Supreme Source. Our decision is thus: do we continue as we have done, maintaining the integrity of the earth as best we can? Or do we rouse the clans and confront the Impostor and his minions in order to bring peace to the earth and guide Man back to the Source?'

For a while none of the Faeries dared to speak. Then from the back of the crowd a voice rang out. 'Our time on the earth has been characterized by great joy.' It was Litanya Emberglow of the Fire clan who spoke. 'We have been entranced by the beauty of creation and have laboured to see it reach its full fruition. Yet the most pleasing of all things I have experienced on this earth has been

Litanya Emberglow

Nalarra Smokewisp

the sound of human voices raised in praise to their creator. In these troubled times it is a sound I seldom hear.'

She paused, and the Faeries muttered in agreement.

'Our primary task is to guide Man back to the Supreme Source and Maker of All Life,' she continued. 'It is a task that grows more arduous as the Faeries of Chaos lead him to ever deeper levels of depravity. It is my belief that unless they are stopped, our purpose on the earth becomes meaningless. I say we confront the Faeries of Chaos for the sake of the earth and of Man!' she cried finally, and the Faeries around her took up the chant.

'The earth and Man! The earth and Man! The earth and Man!'

Ashreyel bowed his head in acknowledgment. 'So be it,' he said, his voice heavy with despair. 'For the sake of the earth and of Man.'

The Great Struggle of the Faeries

The resulting conflict, known as the Great Struggle of the Faeries, has raged for many years, even to this day. At times it appears as though the Faeries of the Impostor will claim dominion over the earth, and at others, the Faeries of Ashreyel hold the upper hand – then, for a while, peace reigns.

But there came a time when Faeries of both sides grew weary with the constant battle for dominion. The Impostor realised that the spirits of his Faeries of Chaos would soon be broken by the relentless incursion of the Faeries of Ashreyel, and he began to hatch a new plan. Eventually he sent for Daecien Darkmist, and together in the Impostor's cave, deep within the Mountains of Sorrow, they talked and plotted. Soon the Impostor summoned all of the Faeries of Chaos to the great underground cavern, and when all were present, he addressed them.

'The clans of Chaos and the Faeries of Ashreyel appear evenly matched,' he declared, 'and

Atarae Lavenderbalm

neither can win outright victory. Our mission to rid the earth of the scourge of Man is frustrated by this constant battle for supremacy. This, therefore, is my command: you must travel the earth and collect the essence of each cruel and wicked deed you discover. Hoard the spirit of the silt and effluent from the rivers, gather the torment of the polluted skies, assemble the last cry of every creature tortured or killed by Man. Every heinous deed and horrifying brutality, every act of spitefulness and harsh word, find them and bring them to me.'

When the Faeries had left to do his bidding, the Impostor turned to the one who stood concealed in the shadows of the cavern. 'There can be no turning back now,' he said. Daecien Darkmist stepped forward into the half-light, and on his face there glowed a wolfish smile.

Over the days and nights that followed, the Faeries of Chaos scoured the earth for the miserable, the maimed and the sick. They gathered the grief and vile malevolence of all ages, harvesting it carefully so that not one grain of sin or guilt was overlooked. Then, laden with their spoils, they returned to the Mountains of Sorrow, where they emptied the fruits of their labours into a huge vat and allowed them to steep together, the mixture swirling with a life of its own, so oily and viscous that light could not penetrate its surface.

At midnight, the Impostor and Daecien Darkmist cloaked themselves and left the cavern, bearing with them a crystal phial containing the distilled essence of all the evils of the world. In silence they made their way to a nearby town, where the fire of a forge still glowed into the night. At its door stood a man awaiting their arrival. Although clearly discomfited by the presence of the Faeries, his greed shone in his eyes as he held out his hand for the payment that had been promised him. Daecien handed him a heavy bag, which was pocketed swiftly. Then, with a mocking bow, the man welcomed them into his forge, where the furnace blazed white hot.

The Impostor's lips tightened in excitement, and although no word was spoken, the two Faeries drew near to the fire with one accord and gazed as though mesmerised into its glowing depths. As they watched, the man took up a pair of tongs and withdrew a sword from the furnace, placing it carefully on the anvil before taking up his hammer to beat the metal. When he deemed the sword perfect, he gestured to the Faeries to admire his work.

Daecien and the Impostor stepped closer. From the sleeve of his robe, the Impostor brought forth the phial, and as the man drew back in dismay, he uncorked it and spilled the contents onto the scorching metal. With a hiss like the screaming of a tortured soul, the blade took on a dull black sheen, as though it was made of obsidian. A violent wind blew around, and in the quiet that followed, Daecien stretched forth a hesitant hand to pick up the sword. Its hilt fitted his hand as though it had been designed solely for him, and he held it aloft, laughing exultantly.

His laughter was echoed by the smile of the Impostor. 'The Sword of Lament!' Daecien declared triumphantly. But as he turned away, he missed the sardonic look in the hooded eyes of the Impostor that had replaced the seemingly innocent smile.

The Sword of Lament

The Impostor knew that the Faerie clans united around Ashreyel the Wise, and in this knowledge lay the seed of his plan. He reasoned that if he could remove Ashreyel permanently from the side of good, then his Faeries of Chaos could seize their opportunity to rid the world of Man. He knew too that he would have only one chance to destroy Ashreyel, and thereby throw the Faeries into confusion and dismay.

Faeries are impervious to physical weapons, but the Impostor's weapon was created of far more potent material than iron, forged as it was from the essence of the evil of the world and fashioned by Man and Faerie in one accord. This potent combination had shaped a weapon that possessed a greater might than the ability to convey mere death. The Sword of Lament embodied the power of Unmaking, the ability to disperse the being of a Faerie into the individual elements of which he was comprised, eliminating him for ever from the face of the earth.

The Impostor knew that Ashreyel was seldom without Faerie companions to protect him. Thus the only method he could use to rid himself of his enemy would be guile. For many years he had been cultivating the friendship of Daecien Darkmist, who had once been Ashreyel's closest companion and confidant. Now Daecien had bonded himself to the Sword of Lament, and the Impostor knew that its heady presence would burn its way through the Faerie's spirit, filling him with a sense of power that he could only experience at the touch of the sword. In this way the Impostor guaranteed Daecien's compliance, even though he did not doubt his loyalty to their cause.

Judging the time to be auspicious, the Impostor gathered up the sword in its scabbard and made his way to where Daecien Darkmist had his haunt, at the top of the Crag of Desolation, where sickly lichens and forest weeds clung precariously to the weather-beaten rocks. Before making his presence known, the Impostor watched in amusement as Daecien paced up and down on his ledge like a caged animal, his frustration and his longing for the sword evident in every movement of his agitated body.

'Daecien,' the Impostor called softly, and Daecien jumped as though stung. When he saw the Sword of Lament hanging loosely from the Impostor's hand, precariously close to the edge of the lofty crag, he gave a small cry, and held out a beseeching hand. 'I have a small gift for you, Daecien,'

Daecien Darkmist

the Impostor continued casually, holding out the sword to the wild-eyed Faerie, who took it slowly and unbelievingly. 'While this blade is in your hand, you are impervious to any attack. It is your bonded slave, the might of your arm. In it resides the power of Unmaking, yet it will not harm you while you bear it in my cause.'

As Daecien Darkmist's hand closed around the hilt of the weapon, the feeling of invincibility he had first experienced in the forge flooded him once again, and it was a different Faerie who now stood facing the Impostor, tall, proud and unbowed.

'I have a mission for you,' continued the Impostor, making his voice light yet deliberate.

'You have but to name it, my liege,' said Daecien, and he meant every word.

'I would have you raise the Sword of Lament against Ashreyel,' declared the Impostor. At this, Daecien blanched and turned away in confusion. 'Come now, Daecien,' said the Impostor. 'You knew that the sword was forged to Unmake Ashreyel in order that the Faeries of Chaos might rule the earth. You yourself were part of the process.'

'I knew,' countered Daecien, 'but I never thought that I would be the one to strike the blow.'

'But who else would be able to approach Ashreyel as easily?' asked the Impostor quietly. 'You are the only one he would trust. It must be you.'

'I was his comrade once, and the Mirror of his Being,' whispered Daecien. 'No matter how I despise him now, I cannot change that fact.'

'Ah, well,' said the Impostor regretfully. 'I suppose I will have to find another to wield the Sword of Lament against our enemy.' He held out his hand.

If Daecien had been pale before, he now grew even paler. 'I will not give up the sword,' he said.

'But it was forged for that purpose alone. I cannot let its power be dissipated through your selfishness,' said the Impostor harshly. 'Give it to me now!'

Daecien Darkmist's inner turmoil was plain to see, as memories of his friendship with Ashreyel warred with the hatred he now felt for the other Faerie and desire for the power of the sword. He remembered the last conversation he had had with Ashreyel, when he had felt his friend's disapproval and disgust, and eventually his darker emotions won. 'Leave the sword with me,' he told the Impostor.

The Impostor nodded calmly and turned to leave. His face bore a fierce look of triumph, yet Daecien Darkmist did not see it, for his eyes were fixed firmly on the obsidian blade.

The Destiny of Daecien Darkmist

For many days Daecien Darkmist did nothing with the Sword of Lament save admire its deadly beauty. He could not bear to face the decision he had made, yet was unwilling to give up the weapon that gave him power. Although Ashreyel had become his sworn enemy, there was a small part of Daecien that admired the other Faerie's fortitude and inner strength. Regret for the friendship that had been lost entered his mind at times, yet he pushed away his doubts, comforting himself with the knowledge that the earth would be better for the loss of Ashreyel, his Faeries and, ultimately, Man.

The Impostor said nothing to Daecien during this time, yet secretly he was poised as though on a knife-edge. He wished with all his might to be witness to this event, and so when a cloaked and hooded Daecien Darkmist left the realm of Chaos to journey to where Ashreyel held council, the Impostor followed him, unseen.

Ashreyel the Wise

For many days Daecien journeyed, until at last he came to the great tree, Wisewood. As he had expected, Ashreyel was standing beneath its spreading branches, communing with the nature around him. The autumn leaves were falling as the tree readied itself for the long sleep of winter, and the sunlight caught their myriad colours as they eddied around Ashreyel's motionless figure. For a long time Daecien lurked in the shadows, watching his erstwhile friend who appeared to him at once so familiar and yet so foreign.

'Would you not rather join me here in the warmth of the autumn sunlight, Daecien?' asked Ashreyel quietly.

Daecien started violently. It made him angry that Ashreyel had been aware of his presence, and with barely a hesitation he made his way out of the gloom into the dying rays of the sunlight. There he turned to confront Ashreyel.

'You are changed, Daecien,' commented Ashreyel, gazing searchingly into the face of his once-beloved companion. Years of dwelling in caves and on clifftops, listening to the malicious words of the Impostor, had warped Daecien Darkmist somehow, twisting him as surely as the stunted trees that grew near his lair on the crag.

Daecien acknowledged the truth of these words, and the pronounced difference between himself and Ashreyel, who stood tall and straight before him, fired his resentment.

'Still so proud,' he hissed. 'But all your arrogant righteousness has won you nothing, Ashreyel. If you had but worked with us instead of against us, you and I could have ruled the world.' With these words he felt the Sword of Lament pressing against his back as though alive and hungry, and he was consumed with an almost irrational urge to draw it.

Ashreyel smiled a desolate smile and turned away, looking up into the stark branches of Wisewood. His lack of regard angered Daecien further, and in one swift movement he drew the black sword from its scabbard. In that instant he felt energy flowing into him, thrilling him to the depths of his being and strengthening his resolve. He pointed the weapon at Ashreyel's exposed back. 'Have you not learned, Mirror of my Being,' he said bitterly, 'that in this world you must either conquer and rule, or lose and serve? You can be the hammer or the anvil.'

'You show a strange desire to seek power, but by gaining it you lose your freedom, Daecien,' said Ashreyel with heartfelt compassion. He fell silent, lost in thought. 'When did you learn to hate me?' he asked finally, as he turned to face Daecien again. The point of the Sword of Lament hovered close to Ashreyel's breast, and he was unprepared for the evil he felt flowing from it. He staggered back, knowing instinctively that the sword held power greater than he had experienced before, and he regarded Daecien warily.

'I have loved you too greatly not to hate you, Ashreyel,' answered Daecien, shocking himself with his sudden honesty. The weakness infuriated him, and he nudged the tip of the sword closer to Ashreyel as he continued. 'Why did you come to the Wisewood Tree unprotected? Why are you alone here, Ashreyel?'

'I knew you would be here,' Ashreyel admitted quietly, unable to take his eyes from the obsidian length of the sword, 'and I wanted to meet with you alone.'

The compassion in Ashreyel's voice made Daecien look up at him. He was amazed to see tears on Ashreyel's cheeks and, unable to stop himself, he exclaimed, 'I have come here to destroy you, Ashreyel!'

'Do you not think I know that?' Ashreyel's voice was heartbreaking in its agony.

'Why then are you here?' Daecien repeated harshly. 'Do you fear me so little that you believe I am no threat to you? Am I so insignificant that you do not even bring your guards?' The sword's control over him intensified, and his anger flared white hot.

'My friend, Mirror of my Being,' said Ashreyel at last, 'why should I fear you? You were with me when I first walked on this earth. Through many years we have shared pain and laughter, tears and abundant joy. We have danced together and mourned together. My heart rejoices to see you again after all this time.'

'Much has changed since the day we parted,' Daecien replied. 'You would not support me when it mattered most. Instead you chose to stand in judgement on my deeds, condemning me for the choices I made. My decisions were taken for the good of the earth – something we had always strived for together. But you abandoned me, while you did everything in your power to foil my plans. For that alone your essence should be scattered to the four winds. But more so for every creature that has been tortured, maimed or killed by Man to satisfy his whims; for every tree cut down heedlessly, for the pollution of the streams where fish once swam and the skies where birds once flew; for every man, woman and child murdered in the cause of war: for these you deserve never to see another dawn.' In righteous anger, Daecien raised the Sword of Lament high above his head, while Ashreyel recoiled in horror from the blow that would bring about his Unmaking.

The Impostor, who had followed Daecien to the Wisewood Tree, surveyed the unfolding scene from the shadows. But at that moment he could contain his malicious excitement no longer, and sprang forth to witness the death of his long-time foe. His eyes glowed viciously with triumph as the blade descended swiftly. Yet as the weapon was about to fall upon Ashreyel, Daecien halted its downward arc, faltering at the very moment of impact. In fury, the Impostor rushed to where the pair stood motionless. 'Go on, fool,' he commanded Daecien. 'Why do you stay your hand? Destroy him and the world is mine!'

'I cannot,' uttered Daecien Darkmist in a dull voice, his eyes meeting Ashreyel's for the first time. 'He is the Mirror of my Being,' and with this he turned away, the Sword of Lament drooping from his suddenly useless fingers.

The Impostor gave a hollow shriek of laughter. 'What fools the Faeries are,' he scoffed, though his face was as white as bone. 'Did you not guess, Daecien, when we forged the Sword of Lament, that its hunger for Unmaking and blood and death would never be sated? The very nature of its construction created a force that cannot be extinguished. Only I, as its initiator, am impervious to its might. It is immaterial whether you use the blade for the Unmaking of Ashreyel. Its hunger will cry out through the centuries, and many, both Man and Faerie, will feed its desires. The vanquishing of Ashreyel was to be but the first, and most enjoyable, of those demises.'

In horror Daecien Darkmist looked down at the Sword of Lament in his hand. He knew that the words of the Impostor were irrefutably true, possibly the first truth he had ever heard the evil one speak.

Motionless, Ashreyel slowly raised his eyes to meet those of Daecien Darkmist. As the two Faeries stared intently at each other, the Impostor made his move. Feinting to the side, he threw himself towards the immobile Daecien, wresting the sword from his limp fingers, then turned towards Ashreyel. His movement was so swift that he was indistinct as he raised the black blade towards heaven in a dark benediction.

Ashreyel, calm in the path of the descending sword, called the elements under his command to his aid. A fierce fire leapt into being, burning white hot, yet the evil in the sword called to the fire's potential for destruction, and the flames leapt, hissing wildly, into the blade, leaving the Impostor unscathed. Next a mighty wind rushed into the clearing, bowing the branches of the Wisewood to breaking point and whipping the fallen leaves into a frenzy. The wickedness of the Sword of Lament sang once again, and the ferocity of the howling wind was drawn into the weapon. Then Ashreyel commanded rain and hail to drench the Impostor and strike him down, but water's devastating power was captivated by the strength of malevolence in the sword and swirled into the blade. The earth heaved underfoot, and cracks opened, yet even the earthquake was dissipated by the sword. In horror, Ashreyel realised that he had used all the weapons at his command, and the Sword of Lament had absorbed and vanquished every one. Seeing his helplessness, the Impostor laughed exultantly and swept the menacing blade towards the darkening sky again.

In that instant, Daecien Darkmist reacted. In one swift movement he flung himself into the path of the sword as the Impostor brought it crashing down. The blade cleaved through Daecien's spirit being and a terrible high-pitched shrieking arose. The sinister sword shattered into countless pieces, some as fine as dust and none bigger than a pin. The Impostor was hurled backwards by the impact, collapsing against the bole of Wisewood, and Daecien Darkmist fell towards Ashreyel, like an autumn leaf fluttering down from the boughs of the great tree. His face registered no pain, only a deep sense of peace.

The Impostor's shrieks of loss and fury went unheard as Ashreyel cradled his companion helplessly. 'Why?' he asked over and over, rocking his friend in his arms, the tears pouring down his cheeks to fall unheeded on Daecien's face.

At last Daecien drew breath. 'I looked into his eyes,' he whispered, gesturing weakly towards the Impostor, 'and in him, I saw myself, the creature I have become. I could not live with the knowledge that such a being would hold dominion over the world.'

The commotion had attracted the attention of other Faeries, and a hostile throng started to gather. Realising that he was outnumbered, the Impostor swiftly gathered up what he could of the remnants of the sword and secreted the splinters in his robes. Then, as the Faeries advanced menacingly towards him, he fled, shouting impotent curses as he swept away.

At his departure, stillness fell on the scene. A sudden wind whipped the fallen leaves into the air, and they spiralled down gently to land on the two motionless figures huddled beneath the ancient tree, cloaking them in gold and red. Ashreyel brushed a leaf from his friend's hair with a trembling hand, and Daecien reached for him. His eyes fixed on the glowing sunset, his hand clasped tightly in that of his truest friend, Daecien Darkmist gasped once more. His being began to glow with the light of a thousand sparks, which flickered and winked out one by one as his spirit grew dim, and he faded gradually from Ashreyel's encircling arms into the elements from which he was made. Finally, his spirit took wing, returning to the Supreme Source and Maker of All Life from which it originated, and all that remained was a small pile of fine earth, which a tiny breeze scattered despondently amongst the fallen leaves.

The worried Faeries drew closer, unwilling to disturb Ashreyel's grief yet desiring to know if

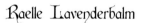

Raelle Lavenderbalm

all was well. In amazement their gaze fell upon the shattered remnants of the sword, and they marvelled at its absolute ruin, for they had realized that it was no ordinary weapon. They began to gather up the splinters so that Ashreyel could decide what to do with them.

At that moment Ashreyel raised his bowed head, and his voice, when he spoke, quivered with anguish. 'Daecien Darkmist's one selfless action was enough to overcome all the evil that resided in the Sword of Lament. He knew that it would bring about the Unmaking of many, and could not live with himself as the instigator of such destruction. So it was that he placed himself in its path, and thereby destroyed it.'

'Why did he not turn it upon the Impostor while he had it in his grasp,' questioned Raelle Lavenderbalm, 'and thereby remove his wickedness from the earth for ever?'

Ashreyel considered her question. 'If Daecien Darkmist had attempted to raise the Sword of Lament against the Impostor, the Impostor would not have been harmed, for he was the weapon's master. The sword's thirst for Unmaking and blood would never have been quenched had it been raised against its creator. Only the virtuous actions of Daecien Darkmist were powerful enough to counteract the force of its evil and defeat it.'

The tale of Ashreyel and Daecien had saddened me greatly, and on my next visit to Alarissa, I begged her for a lesson of less emotional turmoil. She smiled in agreement, and gathering a small handful of soil, ran it through her fingers as she began to speak.

The Earth Faeries

The loamy richness of the soil inspires the Earth Faeries to create floral bowers deep in the forests where no human eye will ever see them. They comfort the mice babies when their mother is out finding food, and whisper affectionate words to the blind moles and the worms who industriously tunnel the soil. Their capable hands provide healing herbs and plants to injured animals.

Raelle Lavenderbalm's clan has the herbs and flowering shrubs of the garden at its disposal. To these Faeries belongs the perfume of crushed lavender leaves in the summer rain, of basil and thyme flowering under the heat of the sun, of full-blown roses strewing their petals carelessly on the ground. Their busy hands orchestrate the opening of flowers in the morning light, and they mix healing potions from the array of fragrant herbs at their command.

Deep within the loamy richness of the forest is where Chrystann Leafshimmer's clan has its abode. There, in the gloom of pine-scented coverts, the Faeries of the clan labour to bring forth the sweet fruits and rich acorns that will feed the hungry forest creatures. Dusky blackberries, rich with aromatic juices, hang like jewels in the midst of the thorny thickets, and the air is filled with the tang of ripe berries, the woody loam of decaying leaves and the green smells of fresh shoots.

Caerlena and Karyssa Fenmire's clan makes its home in the marshes, surrounded by still water and abundant bird life. Here, the marsh warbler's cries float eerily across the water like the sighs of

lost lovers and bare trees raise pleading arms towards the heavens. Their abode is wild, untamed, mysterious, filled with the aromas of mud and weed, the dark and heady scent of still waters and sensuously twining roots.

Deep in the thickets, the Faeries of Bayarde and Reyah Nutbrown have their domain amid thick tree-trunks, the moss-covered homes of fantastic fungi and hanging lichen, venerable woodland giants festooned with wreaths of ivy and trailing creepers. Here the earth is carpeted with thick layers of fallen leaves, cushioning the footsteps and crackling with dry twigs. It is a place of musty scents and sleepy sunlight, of the sharp, fresh tang of new-fallen snow lying heavy on creaking branches in winter, and of warm burrows for small forest creatures.

Bayarde Nutbrown

Chrystann Leafshimmer

overleaf: Karyssa Fenmire

Monday, 24th November 1664

I have noticed on my trips into the town of Winston lately, that the local gentlewomen have been gathering in gossiping huddles, clearly enjoying some sort of conspiracy. At first I was amused by the secrecy, but eventually my curiosity achieved the better of me, and today I bustled loudly into one of their informal meetings in the town square.

'Who would like to tell me what is going on?' I asked outright, pleased to see many of them start guiltily.

Dame May, a portly matron in widow's black, answered unconvincingly, 'Why, nothing, Dame Kellerman.' I could see she was bursting to tell me their secret.

'Pish,' I retorted. 'I demand to know what has affected the women of this town to such an extent that they stand around all day cackling like hens in a coop!'

Dame May faced the group. 'Surely we can tell her?' she asked them tremulously, and a few nodded their heads. Immediately she drew me closer into their circle until I could feel the breath of all the ladies on my cheeks. 'There have been mysterious goings-on in Winston lately,' she uttered cryptically. A heavy silence fell, as though none was prepared to say any more.

'Oh come,' I said, exasperated. 'I have helped to deliver four of your children. Surely you can have nothing to hide from me?' Dame May blushed, and thin Dame Wood took up the tale.

'There have been sightings of a ghost in Winston,' she whispered, so low that I struggled to hear her.

'A what?' I asked loudly. 'A ghost, you say?' Hurriedly the women shushed me, looking about wildly for any sign of my having been heard.

'I was the first to see it,' said Good Dame Edna proudly, and the other women nodded conspiratorially. 'It was late at night, and I thought to check whether the hen coop was closed for the night. I made my way outside in my nightgown, carrying only a candle. As I stood on the threshold, a sudden gust of wind blew out the candle, leaving me in the darkness with only the crescent moon to light my path. Thinking nothing of it, I left the candle stub inside and went out into the garden.' Her voice grew hushed.

'Carry on, Edna,' whispered one of the women eagerly.

'Oh hush, Mary,' another urged. 'You have heard this tale a thousand times before!'

I glanced fiercely around the avid circle and the quarrelling ceased. Dame Edna gave me a swift look of gratitude. 'As I was saying,' she continued, 'I was just straightening up from checking the coop when I saw it.' She paused for effect. 'A figure loomed out of the forest and made its way into the town. It was a ghost,' she ended dramatically, and all the other women cooed in agreement.

'Are you sure, Edna?' I asked impatiently. 'A sheet flapping on a line in the dark could easily take on the aspect of a malicious spirit.'

'It is not the only sighting, Dame Kellerman,' said Dame May. 'There have been others.'

'Such as?' I queried, regretting the question even as I asked it.

'Master Barnes, who owns the grocer's on Darby Lane, had all of his fruit turn bad in one night. His dog, normally chained up behind the place, was unaccountably missing, the lock sprung open, though I am sure the poor thing is better off without him, he was so cruel to it.' A bell rang somewhere in the back of my head. I felt I knew the truth of their ghost, but I said nothing.

Dame Smythe spoke up. I had recently heard a rumour that her husband's fists found their mark on her face on many an occasion, and I pitied her. 'My husband is fond of a tot of an evening,' she began timidly.

'Aye, when the wine is in, the wisdom is out,' muttered Dame May snidely.

Dame Smythe continued without appearing to notice the interruption. 'One evening last week he was lying beside the fire after I had gone to bed, when, he swears on his life, a strange being loomed up out of the coals to stand in front of him. The being was made all of flame, and it looked at him with piercing eyes and spoke in a terrible sepulchral voice. It laid a hand on his head, and where the fingers touched, his hair turned silver-white. I do not know what the being said to him, but afterwards my husband came to me on his knees to beg my forgiveness for his ... harsh treatment. I believe it was the same ghost that accosted him that night.'

The other women were speechless with envy for a moment. Then other stories followed thick and fast, and all the tales had in common the sighting of a strange being. At times it was merely a pair of eyes that gazed with wry amusement from the depths of a fire; at others, a fleeting glimpse of a shadowy figure.

I had heard enough. I left the group chatting animatedly and headed home. I was sure that I knew what was happening in Winston, and I barely stopped at my cottage before taking the path to the Pool of Half-Remembered Dreams.

Alarissa laughed heartily as I related the stories of the woes of the evil-doers of Winston. 'It appears that Tirra is at her favourite pastime again,' she declared, and her peals of merriment filled the forest.

'Tirra?' I asked, for I had not heard that name previously.

Alarissa settled herself to tell a tale, and I made myself comfortable.

The Tale of Tirra Flamefrolic

Tirra Flamefrolic had not been guardian to her clan for long when she became restless and curious to experience more of the world, a sensation that often besets Fire Faeries because of their wild and impetuous natures. She began to undertake clandestine journeys of discovery, each more fascinating to her than the last. Faeries are not bound by the laws that govern the physical realm, and are able to appear and disappear at will. Thus she was able to observe the doings of Man in nearby Winston without being noticed herself.

During her investigations, Tirra saw scenes of arresting beauty, and others of shameful corruption that disturbed her deeply. In a serf's hovel she witnessed the birth of a child, and the first gentle kiss his mother bestowed on his downy head. At the fireside of an inn she saw a man pay for a murderous deed with gold. She observed great and noble people committing mean deeds, yet she witnessed the lowly and ignorant perform acts of extraordinary power, and she realised how the smallest action can have far-reaching consequences, like the ripples of a stone thrown into a still pond.

Tirra had never been one to sit idly by, and her Faerie spirit, full of the vitality and brightness

of fire, longed to set things right. Eventually she resolved to take matters into her own hands, and began to visit the town of Winston regularly, inflicting swift and inventive punishment on the perpetrators of evil deeds and rewarding those who did good. In her own singular way, Tirra Flamefrolic was encouraging the citizens of Winston to strive towards good and avoid evil.

Alarissa paused in her narration. 'How is it that the people of Winston have not noticed these happenings before now?' I asked.

The Faerie smiled. 'For many years, Tirra has stayed away from the town. Yet sometimes she cannot help herself, and a spate of hauntings and ghost sightings is usually the result. Her actions are never vindictive, however, and it is in order to try to lighten the burden of the helpless and the oppressed that she commits these deeds.'

I took a different path home, one that ran close to the town. Suddenly I was startled by the sound of footsteps coming towards me. By chance, it was Dame Smythe's husband, and I greeted him courteously, though he did not deserve such, for I remembered his wife's bruised face and browbeaten demeanour. I observed with a certain malicious glee the streaks of white in his once dark hair, and the haunted look in his eyes. He nodded to me, then nervously glanced past me towards the Lightning Blast Lookout Tree. I turned to see what had caught his eye, and at first I could see nothing out of the ordinary. Then, as I glanced away, from the corner of my eye I caught sight of a mischievous figure perched in the branches, seemingly clothed all in fire. When I looked again, the figure had disappeared, yet it had not gone unnoticed by Dame Smythe's husband. He had turned as white as a sheet, trembling all over, and with a muffled oath he took to his heels.

I could not help but let out a small chuckle. I might have been mistaken, but I would swear that I was not alone in my merriment and that my giggle was joined by a tinkling laugh, high as the chirping of the birds. Silently I saluted the invisible Tirra Flamefrolic, before turning to make my way home.

The Tale of Bayarde and Reyah Nutbrown

Bayarde Nutbrown, the guardian of one of the Earth clans, developed a great fascination for the boy he had once saved in the forest. He felt a bond between their destinies, and at regular intervals Bayarde and his clan sister Reyah Nutbrown would make their way to where the boy lived, in a cottage on the edge of Winston. The two Faeries would conceal themselves in the fragrant garden, watching for the boy, and they came to know his family intimately.

The boy had a brother who struggled to walk, his leg twisted and deformed from birth. In the warmth of summer, he was brought out on his pallet to lie under an oak tree, and there he would gaze up into the branches for hours, dreaming of a better life. He was joined by his small, ugly dog, a bristle-snouted, grizzled old hound that was suspicious of the watching Faeries but never alerted the crippled boy to them. The stocky dog would lie patiently for hours next to the bed, its head placed perfectly so the boy could easily stroke its ears or feel the warmth of its breath on his hand. The hound's broken master was the one light in its eyes and the joy of all its days. When the boy grew lonely and was tempted to beg his brother to stay by his side instead of running off with the other village children, he would bravely reach for the comfort of his dog. All this the Faeries were witness to, and they marvelled at the greatness of the boy's spirit and the dependability of the hound.

Soon Bayarde and Reyah Nutbrown had duties elsewhere and were away from the cottage for some days. When at last they eagerly returned, however, both were struck by the quietness and seeming desolation in the air as they approached. Even though the weather was warm, the boy was not in his usual spot under the oak tree. All the doors of the cottage were tight shut, the windows sealed, and the air was redolent with a feeling of mourning and sorrow. Bayarde and Reyah sat on the garden wall, wondering what could be wrong.

'The boy is never inside when he could be lying under the tree and admiring the patterns of the branches against the sky,' observed Reyah. 'There is something amiss.' Yet being Earth Faeries, and fearful of the dwelling places of men, the two were unwilling to go into the cottage to see what had happened.

A faint whimpering sound eventually attracted their attention. They cautiously made their way down the garden path but could see nothing. Then, gradually, a diminutive form became visible under the lavender bushes that grew beside the front door. Faded and indistinct, it was the spirit of the faithful hound. Gently the Faeries coaxed it from its hiding place. Reyah placed her arms around the shivering spirit hound and in their minds she and Bayarde could see and feel the dog's memories and experiences. It showed them its life, from a boisterous puppy, excitedly exploring the garden, to its adoption of the young crippled boy as a more mature hound. The Faeries were witness to its faithful protection of its master, a constant reassuring presence by his side, and they too felt the pleasure of a hand smoothed over a hairy head and the scent of a familiar body hugging it close.

But as time had passed, the dog had grown stiffer and more awkward in its movements, unable to jump up next to the boy on his pallet, more inclined to lie next to the fire and warm its old bones. Its sight grew dim, until its only reassurance had been the small hand continually on its head, comforting wordlessly.

At last, one night, as the stars faded into the first glow of the morning sky, the old dog had felt that its body grew too heavy for it to carry any more, and left it lying quietly by the dying fire, taking with it only the memories of a life well lived, full of happiness and trust, and of deep and abiding love.

The two Faeries absorbed this in silent reverence. Then Bayarde spoke. 'Faithful hound, your time on this earth is done. You have lived a life filled with faith and hope. It is time to make your way to your reward, where you will run and play as though a puppy again until joined by your master at the end of his days. Why, then, do you remain here?'

At his words, the hound grew sorrowful, its tail tucked between its legs and its anguish evident in the violent shivers that shook its tiny spirit body. The Faeries suddenly understood that the dog, ugly and insignificant to all but its master, had stayed faithfully at the boy's side, even though parted from him by death. Yet the animal knew that its master still sensed its spirit nearby and pined for his loyal companion. Anxious for the boy's well-being, the dog could not bring itself to go further than the garden path.

Bayarde and Reyah tried to comfort the hound, but it would not be reassured. Eventually, with much hesitation and sorrow, they took their leave. As Reyah Nutbrown glanced back, she saw the hound settle down, faithful as a small sentinel, its shaggy muzzle directed towards the cottage where its master mourned.

For many days the two Faeries pondered what they should do. At last Reyah had an idea. In the depths of night, they made their way stealthily through the town of Winston, and eventually they found what they were looking for. A large dog lay at the back of a ramshackle house, chained firmly to a bracket in the wall, its eyes dull and uncaring, and its ribs showing through its mangy coat. Although the night was chill, it had no shelter, and was curled tightly into a ball. Bayarde approached softly, and the hound raised its head wearily, yet made no sound.

'I greet you, Prince among Hounds,' said Bayarde tenderly, placing a gentle hand upon its head. In that instant he received the impressions of a life of beatings and shame, aggression, pain and hunger. 'I have found you a master who is worthy of you, and of your great heart, if you would have him,' he continued.

The young hound was reluctant, for it was in its nature to be faithful to its owner. 'Your master is undeserving of your confidence in him,' explained Reyah. 'There is another, one who needs you for companionship and love. Come with us.'

With a touch of her fingers the lock sprang open and the dog was freed. Hesitantly at first, and then with growing assurance, it followed the Faeries through the town to the cottage where the crippled boy slept. By now the sun was rising and the glory of the new day edged its fingertips over the horizon. The Faeries led the hound down the path through the lavender bushes and they were met by the spirit of the old dog.

'We have brought you one whose heart is as great as your own, little one,' said Bayarde, kneeling down to the spirit dog. In that instant they were aware of the old one's fears, racing through its mind. Would it be forgotten? Replaced in the affections of the boy? Should this impostor be allowed to take its place? Then into its mind stole an image of the crippled child weeping inconsolably beside the body of his faithful companion, and the dog's mind and heart were stilled. Quietly, with resignation, the old dog moved forward and touched its spirit nose to that of the other hound in acceptance.

What passed between them at that moment, the Faeries did not know, but the young hound lifted its head, baying once, long and loud, to the brightening sky. In the cottage, the boy raised his head from his pillow, then climbed slowly from his pallet. He made his painful way to the cottage door, opened it and looked out to where the thin and mangy dog stood illuminated in the first light of the sun: beaten, but unbroken in spirit. Boy and dog regarded each other silently for a while, and understanding seemed to flow between them, as the Faeries and the dog spirit watched from the shelter of the lavender bush. Then the boy beckoned, and with one accord master and hound turned to enter the cottage together, a small hand grasping the dog's rough coat for support.

Yet on the threshold the boy paused and looked out once again at the garden. It might have been a trick of the light, but for a brief moment he imagined that he saw his grizzled, beloved old dog sitting there, its stumpy tail thumping the path, its form silhouetted against the dawn. Then the image faded slowly from the child's sight. 'Thank you,' whispered the boy into the hush of the morning. He and the young hound turned and made their way into the cottage, closing the door behind them.

It is certain the old dog entered into the reward it had so faithfully earned. I like to believe that when the crippled child goes to his eternal rest, he will be greeted with resounding barks of great joy, and together the boy and his dogs will run like the wind through the evergreen fields.

Reyah Nutbrown

Friday, 28th November 1664

'I have discussed all elements but one with you,' Alarissa said this day, and her eyes glowed. 'The last is that of fire.' I settled myself and listened carefully to her words.

The Fire Faeries

Equipped with tempers to match their chosen element, but fiercely loyal, Fire Faeries are immune to the fire's heat, sometimes impishly encouraging a small coal to jump out of the grate to singe a rug. However, they never act vindictively, and are often responsible for saving mortals' homes from perilous blazes.

The Flamefrolics, led by the indomitable Tirra, are most comfortable in the first rush of the crackling flames that consume dry tinder. Their domain is that of dancing fires on a cold winter's evening, of the aroma of savoury broth bubbling in cast-iron pots and bread set to rise by the warmth of the fire. Their delight is to hide amid the logs and white-glowing coals, playing hide-and-seek amongst the darting flames.

Eliyada Smokewisp's clan makes its home in the smoke that curls lazily up from a dying fire, etching its patterns into the warm air. Their joys are a chill afternoon, the glowing blaze of a cosy fire while snow falls gently on the hills, the scent of mulled ale with honey and herbs, and of brewed tea with the tang of spicy lemon, of coals newly burning and flames that leap up inside old brick chimneys. The delicious crackle and sputter of new-lit kindling, and the pop and sizzle of wet resin in pine logs on a hot flame hold them enthralled.

Tirra Flamefrolic

The fearful power of a blazing inferno, consuming all in its path, is the domain of Dyllenae and Ayla Kindleblaze's clan. With fiery personalities, these Faeries are best suited to the bounding flames, the gold-burnished logs and the frescoed embers of fierce blazes. Their homes are filled with the glory of raging furnaces, the piquancy of molten metal in a cosy forge on a winter's day, and the sharp ring of a hammer on an anvil.

Litanya Emberglow's clan is fierce and warlike, fiery as only Faeries born of air and flame can be. In white-hot glowing firewood and logs embellished with blazing bark they make their homes, glorying in the heat of the smokeless fire. Their adornment comes from the blue flames and jewel-like coals that glitter like precious pearls or opals.

overleaf: Eliyada Smokewisp

Ayla Kindleblaze

'So now I have described to you each of the sixteen clans,' concluded Alarissa. 'The Guardians, together with Ashreyel, were all that remained after the Great Falling Away of the Faerie, and as a reward for their faithfulness to their calling they were entrusted with the stewardship of the elements. As new Faeries have been created, they have gradually made up for those who were lost to the Impostor's deception.'

'What of these Guardians?' I questioned. 'Has none ever been tempted to join the Faeries of Chaos?'

'There was one, once,' admitted Alarissa. 'I will tell you the story of Chrystann Leafshimmer.'

The Story of Chrystann Leafshimmer

When the Sword of Lament shattered, the evil within it remained intact in each of the splinters, every one a potent tool of malevolent intent. The Impostor knew this, and Ashreyel sensed it too, and so it was that the pieces of the sword gathered by the Faeries were hidden carefully, where none could find them and use them for malicious purpose. The remains were concealed in a place known only to Ashreyel the Wise, a place that has since become the site of some of Man's holiest buildings, possibly because of the great sense of power to be felt there even to this day.

The Impostor set about using the small pieces that he himself had managed to gather to their full and deadly potential. A single sliver in the heart of a man made him yearn for war and conquest, for blood and death. Pride, greed and vanity were easily inspired when a minute speck was inserted into an eye. Gossip, slander and rumour thrived where fragments made their way into receptive ears and tongues. And in a mortal heart that harboured a fleck of the Sword of Lament, love died and bitterness flourished.

Man was not the only creature to be affected by the evil contained in the remnants of the sword. The Faerie too had their casualties.

The spirits of Chrystann Leafshimmer and Jaide Leafwhirl had long been intertwined. These two Faeries were of different elements and clans, yet this mattered not at all to them, and it was with great happiness that they spent their eternity together, reflections of each other's spirit. Their bond did not go unnoticed. The Impostor caught sight of the pair in Winston Forest one day, blissful in each other's arms, as they lay under a tree watching the dappled patterns of sunlight cast through the leaves. The Impostor's heart was hardened against the two Faeries, and he decided to wreak havoc to split apart their unified essence.

Unobserved, he crept stealthily closer to the unwary lovers, and slid a spike from the destroyed Sword of Lament into Chrystann Leafshimmer's heart. The change in the Faerie was instantaneous as the evil of the sword worked its way deep into his being, his face growing dark and brooding and his eyes distant. Although he did not perceive what had happened, Jaide Leafwhirl, lying close against his chest, sensed the transformation immediately. 'Is all a'right?' she asked him anxiously,

reaching out to embrace and warm him, his form cold and suddenly unfamiliar against her body.

Without reply, he shook her off and stood up, then he turned from her and made his way through the forest to where the exultant Impostor stood waiting. Jaide trailed him at a distance, crying and begging him not to leave her, for her spirit was bereft of its other half.

'Come, beloved.' The Impostor welcomed Chrystann with a smile. 'The world has seen the last of you in this form,' and he wrapped the obedient Faerie in his poison-ivy cloak and led him unresisting away, while Jaide, realising that Chrystann had been stolen from her for ever, collapsed to the ground heartbroken.

The Impostor guided Chrystann by secret paths where Jaide could not follow to the Mountains of Sorrow, and there the story might have ended had Jaide Leafwhirl not been possessed of strong resolve and even more powerful spirit. Although the other Faeries begged her to let them try to rescue Chrystann Leafshimmer from the Impostor, swearing dreadful recriminations, she stood firm in her view that it would be love, and love alone, that would free him from the power of the sword. She determined that she would not rest until she had found him and returned him unscathed to the Faeries, and to her embrace. Unaccompanied by any other, she embarked on her quest.

For many years she searched for him, knowing that he would stand no chance of redemption unless she attempted to release him. Eventually she came upon the desolate crags of the Mountains of Sorrow, standing like silent monoliths against the darkening sky, and she knew that her long journey had ended. She must surely see him again and she knew that no matter how he had changed, she would recognise his spirit, which would call to hers.

In great stealth she drew nearer to the mountains, for the Faeries of Chaos were everywhere and they would not suffer her to be there if they discovered her presence. As she approached, she could see the Impostor, enthroned on a heap of what appeared to be the monstrous bones of some long-forgotten creature. On the ground by his side lay Chrystann Leafshimmer. The changes in him caused Jaide to cry out in anguish, for where he had once been strong and lithe, he was now pale and sickly, a shadow of his former self.

Her inadvertent cry alerted the Impostor to her presence, and he beckoned her to him with a smile. Unwilling, but resolved to plead for Chrystann, she drew closer to hear the Impostor's words. Chrystann did not even raise his head at her approach.

'How do you like my creation?' the Impostor asked, gesturing to the prone Faerie, and his malicious laughter rang out over the Hills of Despondence and echoed in the Valley of the Bereft.

Jaide did not falter. 'What must I do to free him?' she asked, and the Impostor's laughter was cut off instantaneously.

'This is my suggestion, Faerie,' he spat. 'I will clothe you in mortal flesh, and if you can persuade your companion to look on you with compassion, even for a single moment, I will

overleaf: Chrystann Leafshimmer and Jaide Leafwhirl

125

return him to you in his original form and the spell of mortality will be broken.'

'And if he does not?' quavered Jaide, for she believed she already knew his answer.

'Then you will remain a mortal and die a mortal death,' the Impostor answered calmly. 'And he will be mine, a servant to the end of eternity.'

Jaide quailed inside at the thought of such a choice. Yet her glance rested on Chrystann Leafshimmer, lying heedless at the feet of the Impostor, and her heart was resolved.

'So be it,' she said, and bowed her head in acquiescence.

With a triumphant laugh the Impostor leapt to his feet and spoke the Words of Power. In a flash, Jaide Leafwhirl found herself next to an unfamiliar road in the depths of a winter landscape, an icy wind blowing around her emaciated, rag-clothed body. For the first time since her creation she felt pain, deep, racking pain in all her joints, and her curved spine bent her almost double.

With an ungainly gait that was far removed from her usual graceful stride, she made her way slowly down the road to see where it led. Eventually she came upon a town, gaily lit for the festive season, where muffled and cloaked people hurried about with their arms full of brightly wrapped parcels, as they laughed and gossiped with excitement. Yet every single one recoiled as they passed her huddled figure, turning away or even crossing to the other side of the road. One woman, dressed in rich furs, said to her, 'We have nothing for you here. Go and beg elsewhere.'

Mystified by the behaviour of the mortals, Jaide made her way to the pool in the centre of the town square and stared down at her reflection. Gazing back at her was a horrible apparition: a disgusting toothless hag, with lank and dirty hair hanging unkempt from under a filthy shawl, dirt grimed into every line and wrinkle on her face, and hands wrapped in verminous rags. Numb with shock, the once beautiful Faerie slid slowly to the ground beside the frozen fountain, the Impostor's laughter ringing in her ears.

Somehow Jaide managed to survive the winter, begging for scraps from people's tables, scavenging for food with the thin dogs of the town, sleeping at night with only her own thoughts and the constant dirt and degradation for companionship. Yet she believed that while there was life in her gaunt body, there was some hope.

In the spring, as she sat on the verge of the road where she had first found herself, the Impostor passed with his entourage, amongst them the hollow-eyed Chrystann Leafshimmer. Her lover showed no sign of recognition, not even when the Impostor crowed malevolently at her. 'Where is the beautiful Faerie now?' he mocked. Jaide Leafwhirl despaired at the changes wrought in Chrystann, yet she could do nothing except gaze at him pleadingly, and

Jaide Leafwhirl

fall hopeless beside the road as he turned away unmoved.

Many years passed, and the crippled old hag became more bent and broken. Each spring the Impostor and his followers would pass by, accompanied by the captive Chrystann Leafshimmer, and Jaide thought desperately of a way to break the spell.

Yet she grew weaker and weaker, and one year, as she dragged herself out to the road in the weak sunshine, she knew that she would not live to see another spring. For the last time she lay by the side of the road, waiting for a final glimpse of Chrystann Leafshimmer, and soon she heard the sound of revelry as the Faeries of Chaos drew near.

When he saw her broken and battered body, the Impostor stepped closer, blocking out the sun, taking away what little warmth it gave her. 'Not so proud and confident now, my beauty,' he whispered. 'How does it feel to fail? The time has come for you to look your last on the essence of your being, and to take the image of his servitude with you into death.' With this he jerked Chrystann Leafshimmer forward, making him kneel before him. Then he turned, and the procession made its way off down the road, the oblivious Chrystann trailing obediently in its wake.

With all the strength left in her fragile body, Jaide pushed herself up, and in a reedy voice, hardly more than a whisper, began to sing of the forest that had been their home.

Chrystann did not appear to hear her, though she imagined she saw his steps slow slightly. Encouraged, she continued singing, but although her voice grew louder, Chrystann Leafshimmer still followed the Impostor and his horde. Suddenly, however, he stopped and stood motionless, his head raised as though he was hearing a beautiful melody for the first time. Jaide took up the song again, singing of the beauty of the pine-scented bowers that were the haunt of Chrystann's clan.

Chrystann turned and began to make his way hesitantly back to where she sat, filthy and ugly, a small heap of loathsome rags by the side of the road. As he approached, she gazed feverishly into his dead eyes, willing him to show some sign that he remembered their bond. Yet Chrystann simply stood, mouth hanging slackly, arms by his sides, and she realised that like an imbecile attracted by a pretty trinket, his attention had been diverted for but a short while. With this realisation, she laid her tired head down on the sweet spring grass and closed her eyes, too heartbroken even to cry.

Yet as she felt the cold oblivion of Death reach out to embrace her like a lover, she felt a drop of moisture on her cheek, and looked up. A single tear glistened on Chrystann Leafshimmer's cheek, slowly tracing a track down his face.

130

Jaide Leafwhirl

It was at this moment that the Impostor noticed the absence of his slave and glanced back to locate him. The sight of the Faerie kneeling beside the dying old crone roused him to a fury, and he uttered a shriek so piercing in its intensity that the Faeries of Chaos shook. But he was too late. Chrystann's face had assumed a glow of life, as though he had emerged from a chrysalis, vibrant and bursting with exhilaration. He reached tentatively for the repulsive old woman, then cradled her head against his chest, murmuring words of affection. All at once, in a shower of golden sparks, a miraculous transformation took place. The stringy, lifeless hair of the old woman grew shiny and lustrous, wrinkled skin glowed with health, her eyes became bright and her body limber. Exultantly Chrystann Leafshimmer embraced Jaide Leafwhirl, whose tears ran unabated at the intensity of the look in her lover's eyes. It was as though they had never been parted, their spirits merging once more as the Impostor's vicious curses fell unheeded around them. They were never separated again.

Tuesday, 2nd December 1664

Last night I dreamed a dream of startling intensity and vibrancy. I felt I was lying awake in my bed, looking up at the ceiling. The sun began to rise, the light grew more intense, and the beams of the ceiling became the boughs of massive trees, their leaves rustling in a gentle wind. It was warm and I decided to arise. Barefoot and wearing only my nightgown, I made my way through the trees, and it seemed to me as though I was being watched. Before long I reached a clearing, and there, gathered before me in their magnificent multitudes, stood Faeries of every description and clan. As one they turned to face me, graceful as trees blowing in the wind, and on each beautiful face there was a smile of welcome.

My heart was full as I gazed upon them, and tears streaked my face, for I had long wanted to see them. Before now I had only witnessed them through Alarissa's eyes, though I had imagined each one as she had described. Here was the spirited Litanya Emberglow, her eyes fierce as she placed a hand on her heart and bowed to me. Here was Tirra Flamefrolic, mischief shining in her eyes. Everywhere I looked I caught sight of those I had hitherto only imagined: Baydonn Cloudweaver with his mighty feathered wings, Eliyada Smokewisp, Brianda Dawndew, the gentle Bayarde and Reyah Nutbrown, Jaide Leafwhirl and Chrystann Leafshimmer, arms entwined.

And in the midst of the throng stood my beloved Alarissa Fernspray, her face wreathed in a smile so lovely it caught my breath, and her arms held out in welcome.

As I moved forward, their ranks slowly parted, and each Faerie smiled and bowed low, their hands over their hearts, as I passed. Finally the last of them stepped aside to reveal someone I had not dared to hope I would see again. It was Jonathan Shawe, my beloved, parted from me all these long years. He was vibrant and glowing, his hair as dark and wavy as I remembered, his smile crinkling the corners of his eyes, and I felt as though I was coming home after a long journey far afield.

Yet as I moved towards him I became aware of myself, and I looked down to see a bent old woman clothed in a shabby nightgown done up with frayed ribbon, straggly hair as white and wispy as cotton floating down my back. I was shocked and embarrassed. Surrounded by the gorgeous colours and glorious visages of the Faeries, my aged mortal body seemed an affront. My love did not appear to notice as he stretched out his hands towards me, welcoming me into his embrace. Ashamed, I gestured towards my old, misshapen body.

Ancient Bonds

'Leave it behind,' he said gaily. 'You do not need to bear the burden of mortal flesh here. Join me.' Then he smiled, a smile of such poignancy that I almost cried out. But I shook my head, backing away from the group, the edges of the dream becoming less defined the further I moved from the crowd.

'I am not ready,' I called to them. 'Just a few more moments ...'

When I awoke, my cheeks were wet with tears and my heart beat painfully in my breast. I know my time is fast approaching, but I must ensure that the insights I have gained from Alarissa Fernspray are not lost to the mortal world. I will place this manuscript beneath the floorboards, tucked away carefully so that it may one day be found and its secrets discovered. Over the winter, I made a copy of my manuscript, and this I will leave for Albert Durmonte, my faithful friend. I cannot simply leave the discovery of all of my works to mere chance.

As I write, the world grows dimmer: the time has come for the works of my hands to be weighed in the scales of life.

Epilogue

This is the last entry in Good Dame Kellerman's journal, and the story of her final days is not known.

From what I have learned of her through her writing, however, I am sure that this indomitable old woman, who faced the trials of her life with dignity and aplomb, would have mustered the courage to confront her final challenge in much the same way. When I envisage Dame Kellerman, I think of her as that dark-eyed lass of eighteen, full of fun and mischief, sneaking innocent kisses from her lover behind the cow byre.

Although I searched the cottage thoroughly looking for hidey-holes or secret places where she might have concealed the additional manuscript she spoke of, nothing remained for me to find. I hope that one day her other works may come to light, if only to answer the many unanswered questions whirling in my mind.

On my photographic wanderings in Winston Forest, I discovered many items of Faerie attire hidden in the undergrowth. I was fascinated by the beauty, intricacy and earthiness of their designs. I also discovered many functional items, such as chalices and vials for the transportation of ointments, and numerous accessories, and I have included pictures of these for the reader's interest. Needless to say, I replaced each precious item in the position in which I had found it.

1   Sienna trousers and avocado-green waistcoat
2   Cinnabar magnolia-petal suit jacket
3   Sage-coloured vest and leather-leaf knee breeches
4   Distinguished leather-leaf boots with fern trim
5   Short leather-leaf boots
6   Grass-blade belt with twig buckle
7   Satin-leaf undergarments
8   Elegant fossil brooch for cloak

1   Cyan and emerald skeleton-leaf dress, as worn by Cyanan,
    guardian of Water
2   Olive blade-leaf dress
3   Clover-leaf and flower-bell earrings
4   Verdant waterweed bodice with purple flower accent
5   Velvety leaf undergarments
6   Snail-shell pendant with delicately chiselled details

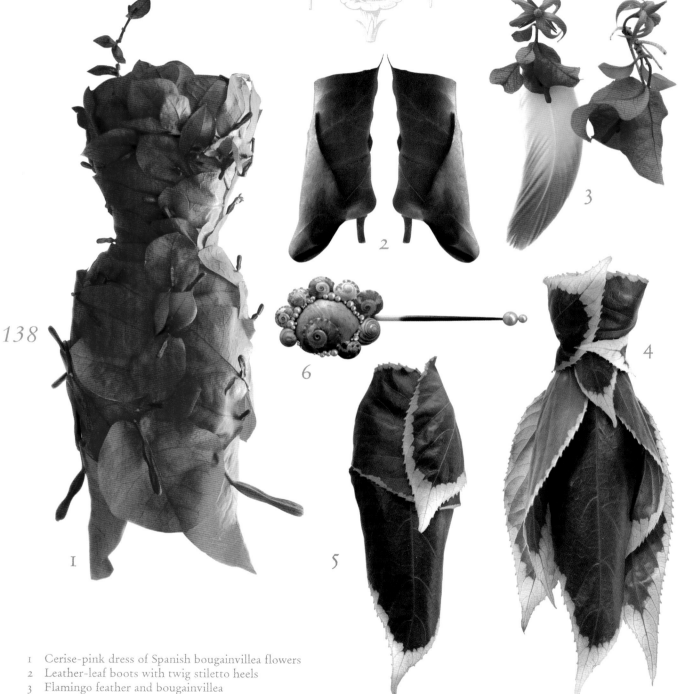

138

1 Cerise-pink dress of Spanish bougainvillea flowers
2 Leather-leaf boots with twig stiletto heels
3 Flamingo feather and bougainvillea
   flower earrings, set in wild tomato flower clasps
4 Striking coral and black leaf dress
5 Detachable skirt
6 Dainty snail-shell and seed-pearl cloak-pin

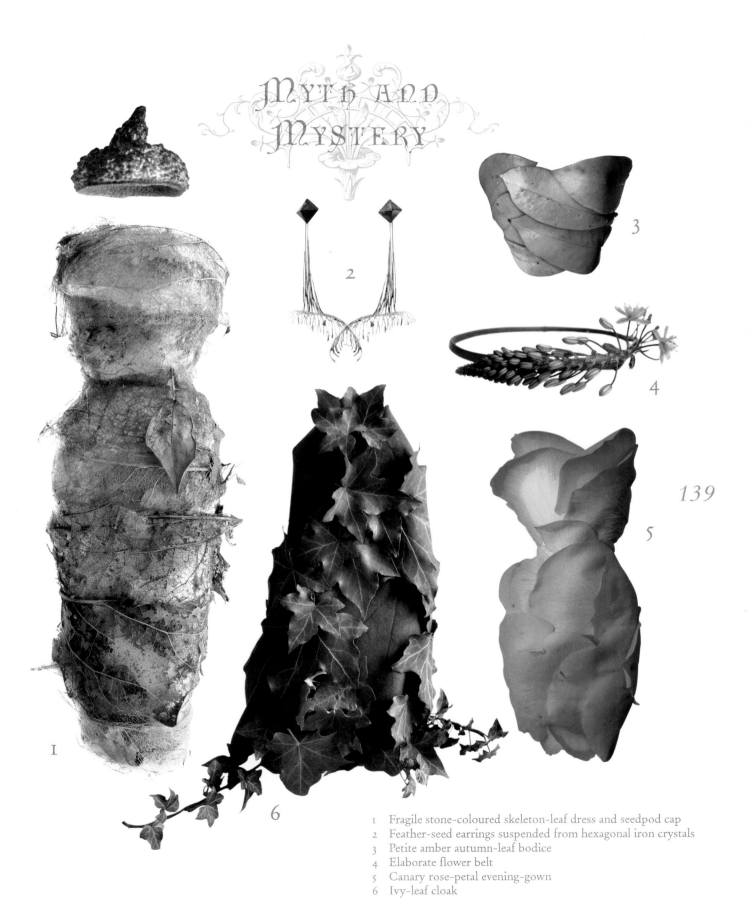

1   Fragile stone-coloured skeleton-leaf dress and seedpod cap
2   Feather-seed earrings suspended from hexagonal iron crystals
3   Petite amber autumn-leaf bodice
4   Elaborate flower belt
5   Canary rose-petal evening-gown
6   Ivy-leaf cloak

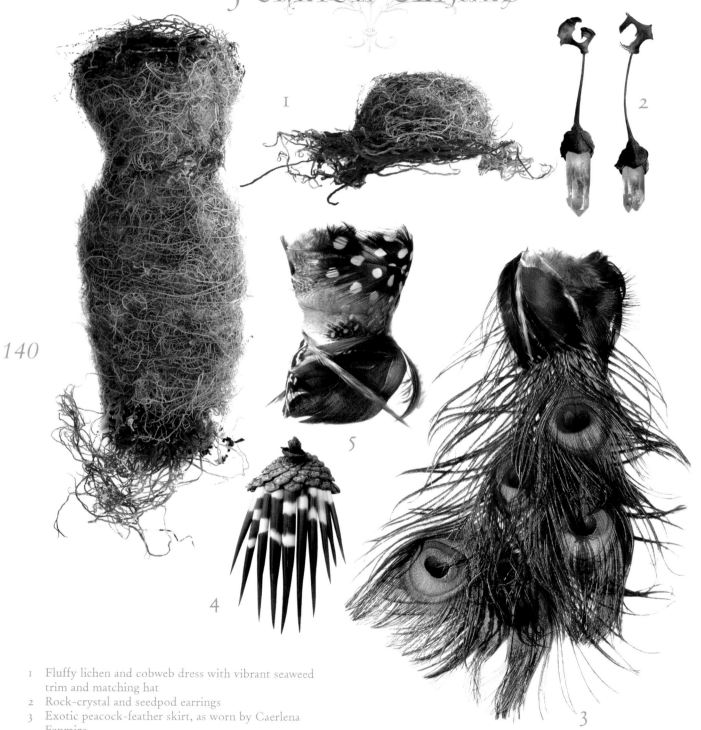

140

1 Fluffy lichen and cobweb dress with vibrant seaweed
  trim and matching hat
2 Rock-crystal and seedpod earrings
3 Exotic peacock-feather skirt, as worn by Caerlena
  Fenmire
4 Quaint porcupine-quill and seedpod hair comb
5 Curious feather bodice with belt detail

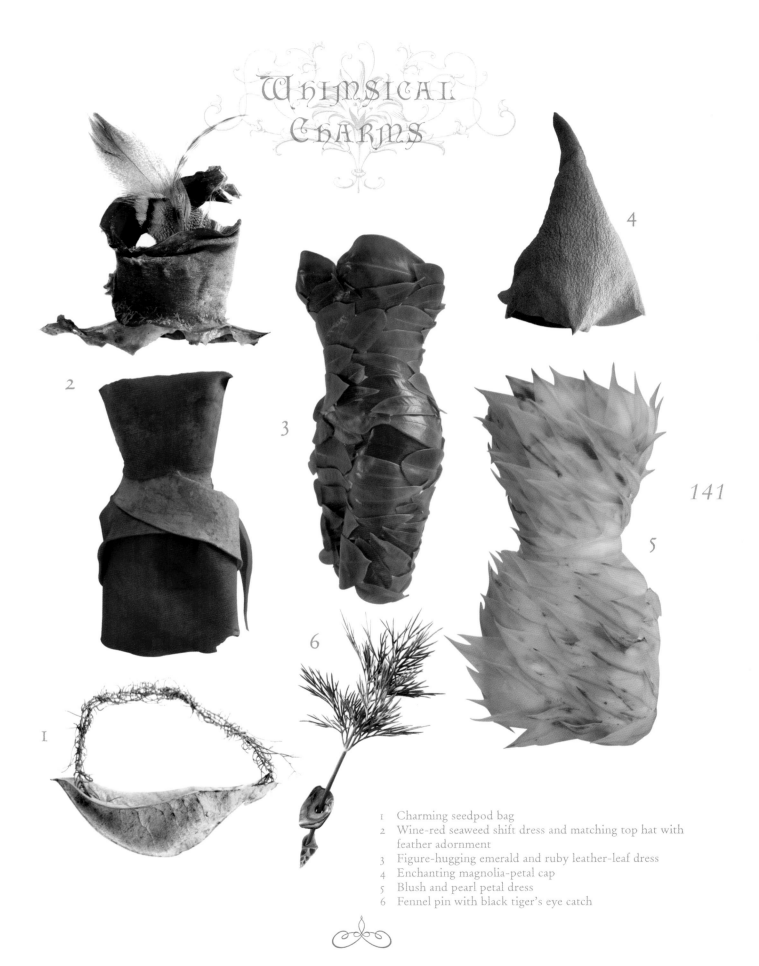

1 Charming seedpod bag
2 Wine-red seaweed shift dress and matching top hat with feather adornment
3 Figure-hugging emerald and ruby leather-leaf dress
4 Enchanting magnolia-petal cap
5 Blush and pearl petal dress
6 Fennel pin with black tiger's eye catch

141

142

1   Fiery poppy-petal dress with ornate matching hat
2   Wispy belt with star-pod buckle and trailing fronds
3   Seedpod cap
4   Ornate leaf evening-gown
5   Shell hair comb with minuscule pearl detail
6   Intricate pearl-pink and coral dress of shells

143

1   Seaweed dresses in cinnamon and olive green
2   Soft petal travelling boots
3   Bindweed necklet with miniature snail-shell
    pendant
4   Flame-flower hat and matching petal dress

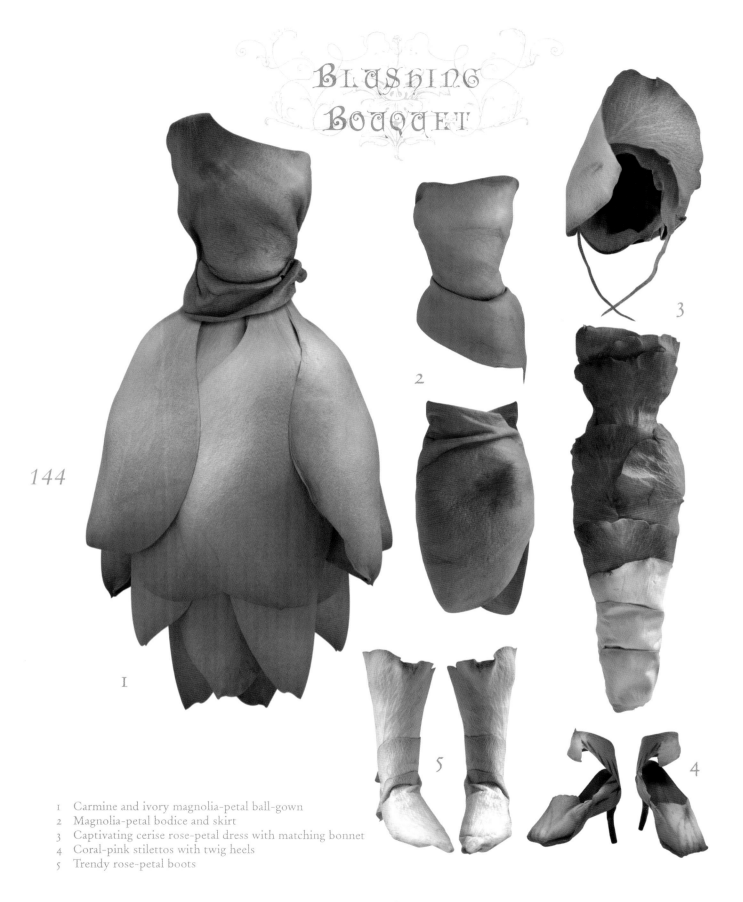

144

1   Carmine and ivory magnolia-petal ball-gown
2   Magnolia-petal bodice and skirt
3   Captivating cerise rose-petal dress with matching bonnet
4   Coral-pink stilettos with twig heels
5   Trendy rose-petal boots

1 Ivy double-caped cloak and rakish hat, as worn by
   Ashreyel the Wise
2 Morning glory ring set with garnet and tiny pearls
3 Seaweed waistcoat and leather-leaf pants
4 Frond vest and matching leather-leaf pants
5 Fossil and seed cloak-pin or brooch

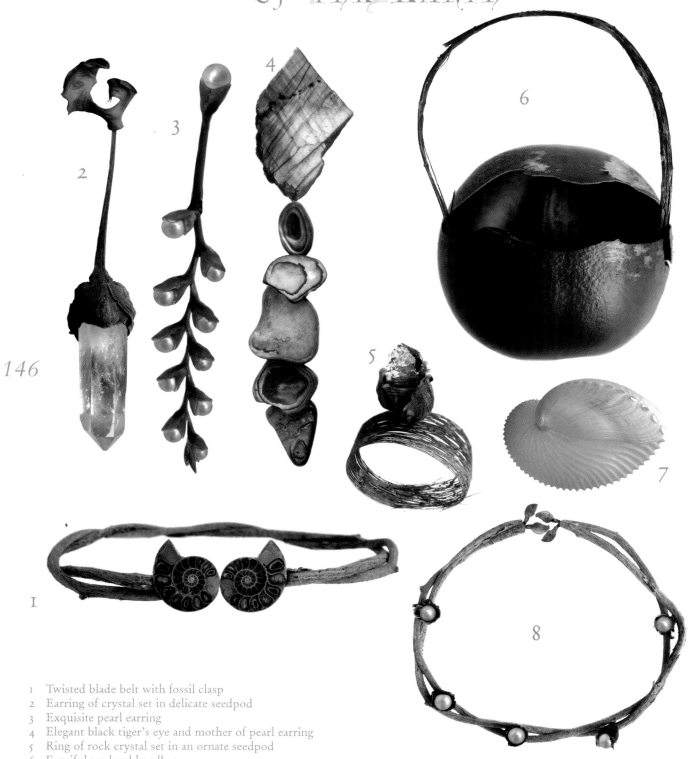

1   Twisted blade belt with fossil clasp
2   Earring of crystal set in delicate seedpod
3   Exquisite pearl earring
4   Elegant black tiger's eye and mother of pearl earring
5   Ring of rock crystal set in an ornate seedpod
6   Fanciful seedpod handbag
7   Abalone and octopus shell belt buckle
8   Tendril necklace with seed pearls and intricate clasp

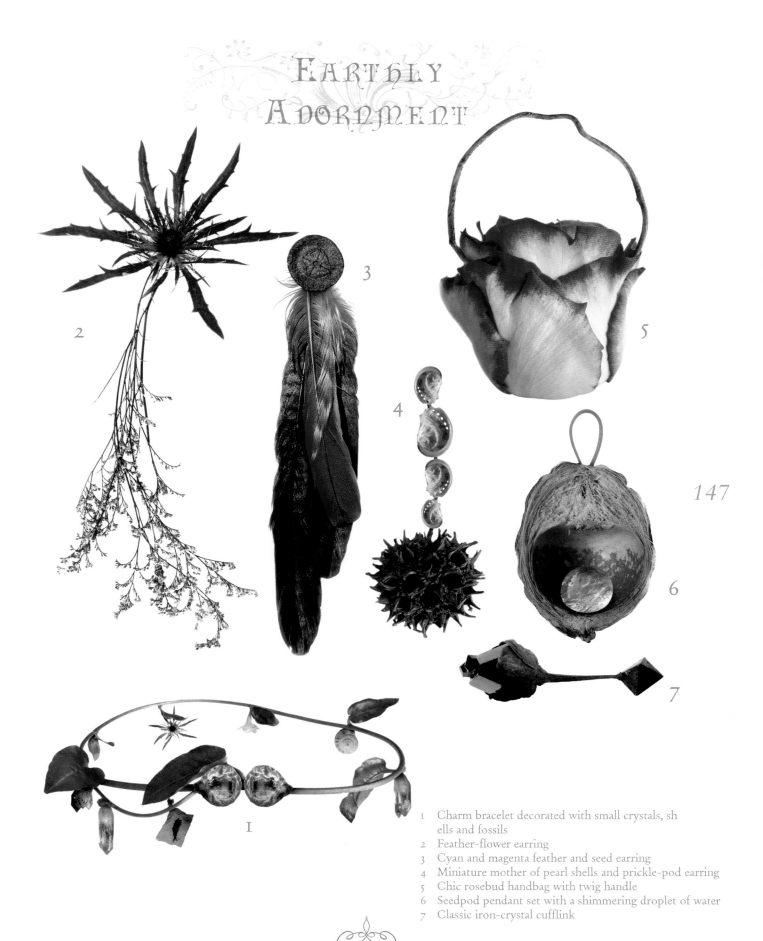

1 Charm bracelet decorated with small crystals, shells and fossils
2 Feather-flower earring
3 Cyan and magenta feather and seed earring
4 Miniature mother of pearl shells and prickle-pod earring
5 Chic rosebud handbag with twig handle
6 Seedpod pendant set with a shimmering droplet of water
7 Classic iron-crystal cufflink

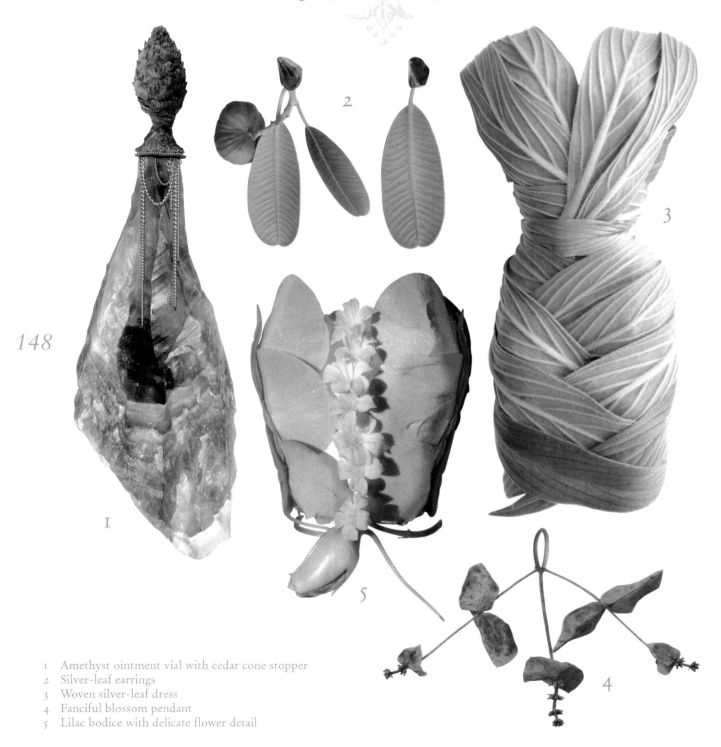

148

1   Amethyst ointment vial with cedar cone stopper
2   Silver-leaf earrings
3   Woven silver-leaf dress
4   Fanciful blossom pendant
5   Lilac bodice with delicate flower detail

1   Richly ornamented dew decanter with seed-pearl
    embellishment
2   Formal vermilion leaf dress
3   Braided ring set with ornamental wild strawberry
4   Delicate flower-stamen bodice

1 Diminutive fuchsia frock in tones of pink and white
2 Delicate crown of sculpted twigs and seed pearls
3 Blossom earring suspended from star-shaped seedpod
4 Flowing hibiscus-blossom ball-gown
5 Crimson leaf earring with furry pod clasp

151

1 Wild grass-seed and leaf dress with wrap-
  around skirt
2 Pearl-encrusted calabash for transport of
  liniment
3 Ethereal, lacy dried-flower dress
4 Playful earring of pearls and seedpods
5 Cheeky fluffy pod shoe with decorative
  heel detail

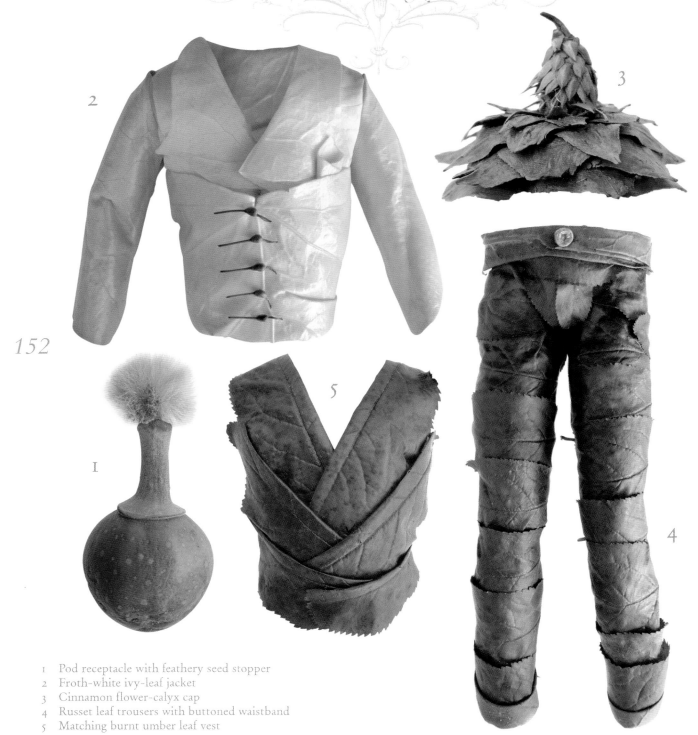

152

1 Pod receptacle with feathery seed stopper
2 Froth-white ivy-leaf jacket
3 Cinnamon flower-calyx cap
4 Russet leaf trousers with buttoned waistband
5 Matching burnt umber leaf vest

2

3

4

1

5

1 Autumn-leaf ensemble with collared
   cloak in rust and olive green
2 Delicate grass-filament cloak-pin
3 Furry headdress with starflower
   ornament
4 Shoe-string strap dress of feminine
   pink and olive green
5 Desiccated autumn-leaf earring

154

1 Ruby leaf nectar chalice
2 Flamboyant frilled burnt orange and sage
   leaf dress
3 Husk hat with fleecy pom-poms
4 Intricate leaf shoes embellished at the toes
   with dangling grass seeds
5 Dainty flower hairpin

1 Pair of leaf shoes with feathery strap accents
2 Close-fitting sienna cap with pom-pom
   embellishment
3 Body-hugging leathery olive dress
4 Vine tendril ring set with pearls and semi-precious
   stone
5 Multi-toned cape with tasselled hood

156

1   Magnolia-petal ceremonial suit with
    pearl-encrusted star-pod breastpin
2   Magnolia-petal ceremonial gown with ivory leaf
    adornment at neck and waist
3   Cream flowerbud dancing slippers
4   Grass-blade belt with fossil buckle

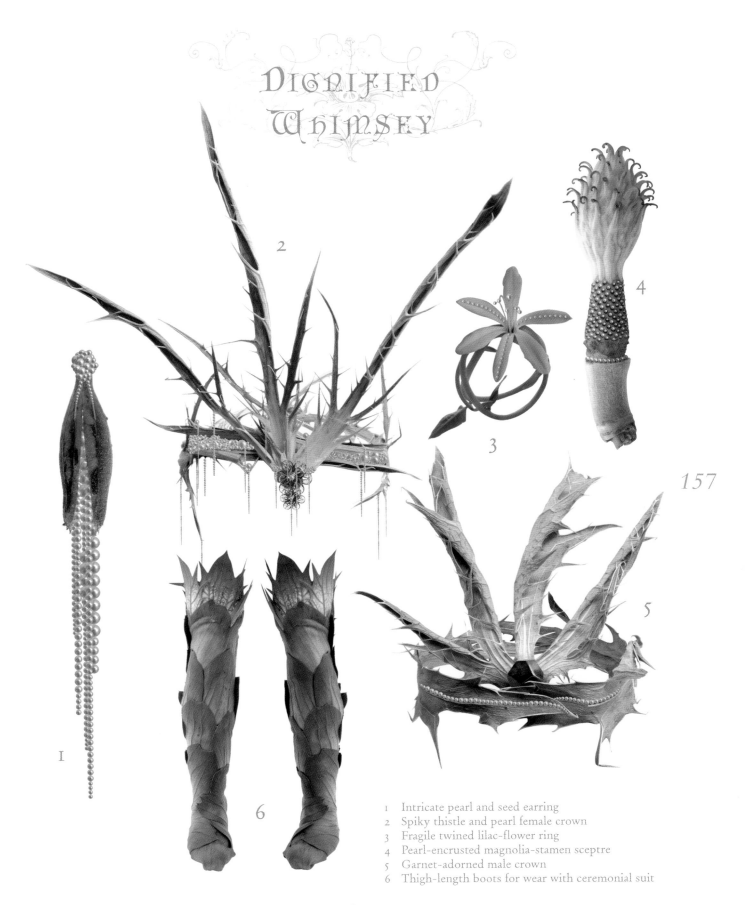

Dignified Whimsey

1　Intricate pearl and seed earring
2　Spiky thistle and pearl female crown
3　Fragile twined lilac-flower ring
4　Pearl-encrusted magnolia-stamen sceptre
5　Garnet-adorned male crown
6　Thigh-length boots for wear with ceremonial suit

158

1 Clover-leaf dress with mauve flower ruffle
2 Rose-petal skirt with ethereal petal bodice
3 Blossom-water vial decorated with pearls and fennel
4 Fanciful earring with daisy-bud clasp
5 Frivolous purple blossom bodice

1 Form-fitting shiny leaf dress
2 Prickly husk cap with pom-pom
3 Sophisticated grass-blade, seed and pea-pod dress
4 Vine tendril and pearl earrings
5 Spiky cone bottle with pod cork

'Across the pages of our lives track countless footprints of those
loved and lost. Here, may they live forever.'

Dame Kellerman 1664